They Told Me
I Couldn't

**A Young Woman's Multicultural Adventures
in COLOMBIA**

TAMALYN DALLAL

FIRST EDITION

TALION PUBLISHING, Renton, Washington

This book is available at a special discount when ordered in bulk quantities. Please see back of book for related publications that may be of interest. To schedule Ms. Dallal for an interview or speaking engagement, contact Talion Publishing.

Talion Publishing
330 SW 43rd St. Suite K-547; Renton Washington 98055, USA
Toll-free (in USA) 1-888-232-1787
Outside the USA, call 1-425-228-7131
Fax: 1-425-228-3965
E-mail: talion@ix.netcom.com
Web site: http://www.talion.com

ISBN: 1-890916-19-6
Library of Congress Catalog Card Number: 97-91279
Author: Tamalyn Dallal
Illustrations by BJ Dudley

Publisher's Cataloging-in-Publication
(Provided by Quality Books, Inc.)

Dallal, Tamalyn.
    They told me I couldn't : a young woman's multicultural adventures in Colombia / Tamalyn Dallal ; [illustrated by B.J. Dudley]. -- 1st ed.
    p. cm.
    ISBN: 1-890916-19-6

    1. Dallal, Tamalyn. 2. Dancers--United States--Biography. 3. Belly dance. 4. Colombia--Social life and customs. 5. Colombia--Description and travel. I. Title.

GV1785.D35A33 1997   793.3'092
                            QBI97-41322

For my father Carl, to whom I will always
be grateful for his untiring enthusiasm.
He encouraged me to share my travels
with others long after I had moved on to
other projects, and his persistence would
not let this book series rest.

I also owe much to Richard Harris, author of many
fascinating travel books, for introducing me to the world
of publishing and taking me to ABA/BEA conventions
long before I belonged there.

I thank my mother Ruth and my niece Erika for their
input and sincere criticism throughout this project.

And I send my love and offer my profound appreciation
to the people of Colombia for their hospitality, and for
allowing me to roam as a free spirit throughout their land.

About the Author ...

Tamalyn Dallal grew up in Seattle, the youngest of five children. She is a member of MENSA, speaks many languages and is renowned for her work in promoting Mid-Eastern dance. Ms. Dallal choreographed dance segments for the 1995 SuperBowl football halftime show, and has since been crowned Miss World Belly Dance.

Her performing credits include dancing for singer James Brown, members of the Saudi Arabian royal family, and even a performance with with Peter Nero and the Florida Philharmonic Orchestra.

Her professional name, Dallal, means "pampered" in Arabic, a description some people contend is not particularly accurate—Dallal enjoys less-than-luxurious adventures and is always one of the first to reach out to needy children.

Foreword

... feminism has nothing to do with hating men – just as belly dance has nothing to do with exploiting women.

"I would *never* buy a book about a woman who exploits herself for a living!" said one publisher. Thinking I'd better eliminate such confusion, I endorsed the title: *Travels of a Feminist Belly Dancer*. Heavens no. People went out of their way to object. "You *can't* call it that. It is impossible for a belly dancer to be a feminist!" they said.

As I think back on how and why I came to call myself a feminist, I realize that it has much to do with independence. It has *nothing* to do with hating men, just as practicing the art of belly dance has *nothing* to do with exploitation of women.

It's just that I can settle for nothing less than the right to think for myself, to go to places I have chosen, to practice the career I most enjoy, and to adhere to standards of personal behavior that give me pride. It is the expectation of these basic tenets of independence, I believe, that defines feminism.

Belly dance, it turns out, is even more misunderstood than feminism. Though the *beledi* originated as a dance by women for women, in celebration of the unity of women, some people confuse it with stripping, which is an entirely different kind of entertainment.

In the Arab world, women often do their partying separately from men, creating their own dances to entertain each

I

other. Uniquely feminine dances have evolved that even include movements to prepare women for childbirth. In an era where people find it increasingly difficult to preserve cultural heritage, the survival of these ancient ethnic dance movements is, I think, a cause for rejoicing.

If you get the opportunity to watch a belly dance show, listen for an instantly-recognizable beat:

dum-dum-teki-tek, dum-teki-tek
dum-dum-teki-tek, dum-teki-tek

In this hypnotic rhythm lies the centuries-old tradition of the *beledi* ("country dance").

Belly dance will dazzle you with a multilayered mosaic, showcasing the folkloric dances of gypsies, farmers and royalty. During the Ottoman Empire, sultans gathered from Central Asia to North Africa, enabling women to fuse their dance forms into an ever-changing art. Abstract dance forms that evolved from these early gatherings can nowadays be seen anywhere from nightclubs to movies to New Age events. Belly dance, in fact, celebrates centuries of feminine self expression.

And about the costumes ...

Traditional *beledi* dancers wore long dresses with a scarf tied at the hips. But a few decades ago Egyptian filmmakers, impressed by glorious Hollywood musicals, reinterpreted *beledi* with two-piece glittery costumes and full orchestration. Like most Mid-Eastern dancers, I perform some of my choreographies in traditional costume and others in two-piece 20th century creations.

Still, it seems an unusual career for an American girl ...

My parents tell me that when I was three years old, I would shut myself in my room and put on every piece of clothing I owned, one on top of the next. By the time I was nine, I designed my own clothes. Fashion has held me spellbound ever since I was old enough to wiggle into new dresses.

Dance, rich and powerful, began to seduce me while I was still in high school. I studied the classical East Indian dance forms of *Bharata natyam* and *Odissi* while working as a dishwasher at an Indian restaurant, and enrolled in classical Persian, modern and international dance classes. But I committed to Mid-Eastern dance because it invited me to design my own costumes, promising me a never-ending supply of sequins.

Yet belly dance did not transition from hobby into career until I learned that it could capture dreams and make them real.

As a child, I memorized colorful photos in the *National Geographic*. Huddling in my room as shadows of evergreens danced upon my walls, I immersed myself in fantasies of visiting such exotic places. From the moment I left the nest, I

wanted nothing more than to step right into those photographs—
but I couldn't. I didn't have any money for offbeat travel in
faraway lands.

My first opportunity to convert those exquisite and
mysterious photographs into real life came in Colombia, where
my ability to dance made many strange adventures possible.

It was in Colombia that I learned to assert my independence. I chose to explore remote locations unspoiled by
tourism, and danced in sparkling costumes that I had designed
myself. Belly dance offered me sequined trails throughout
South America, chock-full of unexpected places, sometimes
filled with unsavory characters.

Arabs Around the World

**Healthy Arabic communities hum along in the unlikeliest
places: Palestinians settled in Bolivia, Haiti and Chile. A
Syrian community flourishes in Brazil. Lebanese entrepreneurs can be found in Nigeria and Mexico. When a Mid-
Eastern dancer pops into town, Arabs visit from miles
around to celebrate.**

*Travel idea: VISTA.
I signed up,
highlighting my dream
destination in pink ink.*

1

By the time I graduated from Kindergarten I had an appreciation for dark eyed boys, which over the years developed into an avid interest in looking at turbaned men on the pages of travel magazines. Needless to say, my first boyfriend was not the boy next door—I chose an Iranian instead, a little wishy-washy type whose only saving grace was being dark and unusual.

I yearned for adventuresome travel, studying faraway lands filled with colorfully dressed people. I couldn't *wait* to get a passport and fill it with stamps!

At parties, when everyone else made a beeline to the living room to blast their rock and roll, I hovered around a group of foreign students, finding their music contagious, the movements that expressed it challenging. One gathering so intrigued me that I practiced hip circles and shoulder shimmies for months. Such was my introduction to Mid-Eastern dance, which soon led me to discover the *beledi*—a word corrupted into "belly dance" by a turn-of-the-century entrepreneur—but *beledi* symbolizes women's unity, not anatomy.

After sampling a variety of universities, studying Farsi, Arabic, French, Sinhalese, Russian and Japanese, I began to plan adventures, trying to come up with a strategy to wander into an obscure culture with interesting music and dance—though the contents of my checking account could sustain little more than my own occasional bounced-check charges. And then I hit upon a plan.

One place captured my imagination. I joined VISTA and requested my desired assignment by highlighting "Zone 10"—the southeastern United States—in pink ink. My dream destination: Appalachia.

"–Wait a minute. You speak Spanish?" exclaimed my VISTA interviewer.

"Yes."

> "Your pay will be low; the conditions of your labor often will be difficult. But you will have the satisfaction of leading a great national effort and you will have the ultimate reward which comes to those who serve their fellow man."
> — Lyndon Johnson, 1964

VISTA

VISTA (Volunteers In Service To America) was conceived by President Kennedy, implemented by President Johnson, targeted for elimination by President Reagan, and merged into the Corporation for National Service by President Clinton.

VISTA workers are not allowed to engage in political activism; nevertheless, VISTA workers helping Appalachian coal miners once upset local authorities so much that they were jailed on charges of sedition.

They switched my VISTA assignment to Miami.

Yuck! I thought. *Everyone is rich there, and probably superficial, too.*

I didn't like it, but nevertheless I hopped on the bus for Miami. Just as I arrived, President Carter declared a state of emergency—Cuba had opened its doors and 125,000 refugees poured out on the Mariel Boatlift, flooding Miami with reasons for Spanish-speaking volunteers. I landed right in the middle of the headline news, surrounded by action and astonishing people—men tattooed from head to toe, rumored to be involved with the Cuban crime underworld; adorable children; hot tropical sun baking new controversies into Miami's social fabric with each new day.

I discovered in Miami an intensely multicultural city, resounding with tropical music and foreign languages (and a few men who merited second glances). When my one-year VISTA commitment ended, I decided not to go home.

The following year I met Kaaren Mils, the opera singer who was to become my mentor.

Coiled on a drift of pending files atop my messy desk was a belly dance belt that I was beading by hand; a stack of food stamps, like box-office tickets to dependency, sat waiting to find new users. I had taken a job as a caseworker for Cuban refugees.

We had a secretary with yellow fuzz-covered teeth who had just left on vacation; she couldn't spell, so I can't say if we were more relieved to bid her good-bye or to welcome her temporary replacement, Kaaren Mils. When Kaaren entered the office, I looked up to see a six-foot-tall voluptuous woman in a platinum blonde bouffant hairdo and full stage makeup, immediately out of place in this bureaucratic office, laughing loud enough to frighten the stockings off of social workers, commanding center stage wherever she went; she wore clothes handmade to fit her large and luscious self, dangling ribbons and flowers.

Though Kaaren sometimes accepted temporary office assignments, she had played Broadway and was once with the Rome Opera in Italy. One could easily envision Kaaren on a stage. Her choice of words always matched her theatrical voice, wonderfully dramatic. When Kaaren described an event, you knew it was an *unbelievably* hot day; the *best* food in New York; the sickest she'd *ever* been.

"Tami, this is the *most* dismal place in the world! You belong on the stage, not here," said Kaaren.

"I'm saving my money so I can travel," I explained. But as she talked I felt a stirring, as if the seed of some exotic tropical plant had suddenly germinated.

"Performers travel more than caseworkers."

"Do you think I can make it?"

"Why not?" she replied. "Is passing out food stamps what you call 'making it?'"

"Well ... no."

"Tami, you should consider taking your dancing to a professional level. Listen, I've traveled all over the world. How do you think I paid for it?"

"How did you?"

"My voice bought the tickets for me," she said.

I knew that day that she had spoken to my soul.

I took her advice and embarked on a career as an entertainer, and a few years later, I found myself on a plane to South America. And this is how it came to be:

One day, out of the blue, an Egyptian musician named Samy called and asked me to dance in Bogotá for a month. At last! A chance to dance my way into some curious and faraway location! I immediately met with Samy and his wife, who was to be the other dancer. But soon afterward Samy called with bad news.

"The job got canceled," he said. "So you can't go."

Then Samy called again with a new idea of his very own. "Perhaps we can salvage the show," he suggested. "I'd like you to audition for me."

"Where?

He named a popular Miami hotel. "Oh yes," he added, "wear your skimpiest costume."

"Forget it."

A few days later, while visiting Sheeba, a ballet and Mid-Eastern dance teacher of some renown who was living in

Miami at the time, we received an odd phone call. Sheeba had oodles of dance videos and a magnificent king size bed, on which I luxuriated, studying Egyptian dancers on her TV. When the phone rang, Sheeba picked it up, glanced at me, and said, "Yes, I have just the one for you. Her name is Dallal."

She turned to me. "Want to dance in Colombia?"

"Tell Samy to get lost. There's no trip to Colombia."

"Yes there is! But not with Samy. It's with Giselle—you know her—and Abe Berry, they're both going."

Abe was a soft-spoken Arabic drummer and Giselle was a glamorous French Canadian dancer. Thinking it strange, after years of dreaming and dropping hints that never culminated in a single invitation to dance abroad, that I should get *two* invitations within a week's time, and still more peculiar that both offers were for Colombia, I decided that this must reflect some sort of inevitability, and that perhaps some portion of my destiny might lie in Colombia.

Giselle and Abe seemed levelheaded enough. Besides, I had just seen *Romancing the Stone* with Michael Douglas and Kathleen Turner, and could hardly wait to see the cute little towns, colorful birds, and folkloric costumes that surely abounded in South America! Excited, I washed all my costumes in the bathtub and laid them out on towels to dry, preparing to achieve my goal: I was going to trek right into the pages of my childhood dreams.

Well-meaning friends hurried to educate me on the

fundamentals of travel in Colombia, like thieves that chop off your fingers for rings. My mother worried about guerrilla revolutionaries so, in my most worldly way, I reassured her that very few guerrillas hang out in Colombia. I met a dancer who had just returned from a year in Bogotá, but all I could get out of her was that Colombian police had kidnapped her husband.

Two days later, terribly nervous, I packed my bags for Bogotá, bringing along a sword, four costumes, and twenty dollars.

Seattle

USA

Miami

CUBA

COLOMBIA

Bogotá

ECUADOR

BRAZIL

Instead of taking us to a hotel, we were taken to a place that was utterly silent, where armed guards patrolled sidewalks, or sat holding rifles.

2

Captured by Bogotá

Giselle looked splendid in fashionable clothes and—heaven forbid—five big expensive rings.

"Take off your rings," I urged, worrying about the fate of her fingers.

She slipped them off and stashed them in her bag. "Is someone meeting us at the airport?"

"I don't know." At 24 years old, I was thrilled from head to toe. My legs began to cramp in the tiny coach-class seats. "Did anyone tell you the name of the place where we will perform?"

"No."

We thought for a moment.

"Do you have enough money for a hotel?" asked Giselle.

"Not really."

The jolting of the plane as it screeched onto the tarmac put a stop to our conversation; we picked up our carry-ons and stepped into South America.

Though I had hoped to land in some fascinating spot, inspired by *National Geographic* and Hollywood, we arrived in Bogotá late at night at a dimly lit airport—no women in sight, but everywhere, men in dark suits. Bureaucrats in cheap dark suits. Businessmen in finely tailored dark suits. The most colorful costumes I saw were khaki uniforms on a horde of machine-gun toting boys.

"This place gives me the eebie jeebies," said Giselle.

"I like dark men," I said.

A government official and a 19-year-old boy whisked us out of the airport. The trying-to-be-mustachioed teenager turned out to be one of my bosses and the official had taken a payoff to help us clear customs—a lucky thing, because customs officials had been instructing me to balance my sword on my head and threatened to confiscate my coin-dangled costumes.

They ushered us into two Colombian-made Renaults. Soon we were rattling along looking at huddles of square flat-roofed houses, all attached to one another.

"Where is the colonial architecture?" I asked, as we passed some high rises.

"Those old white houses? They are downtown–"

"–There's a cow in the street." I tapped the driver urgently. "*Mira! La vaca!*"

The Renault swerved, scattering pedestrians as it caressed the sidewalk.

He didn't miss a beat. "–in La Candelaria, that's where you'll find the old buildings. The historic section."

Instead of taking us to a hotel, the man driving the car

headed into a fancy residential area, utterly silent, where armed guards patrolled sidewalks and sat on front porches holding rifles. If white slavery wasn't a worry before, it nagged at me now.

Expensive homes rubbed up against one another, each modern architect designing his creation flush to the next. Our driver pulled up to a sprawling contemporary one-story mansion and escorted us through a small garden into a huge dwelling, with perhaps fifteen bedrooms surrounding a small interior courtyard. It had a fireplace in its gigantic salon, and four live-in maids.

Two more musicians arrived: an *oud** player from Detroit named Isa, and Karim, a toad-like Moroccan violinist. Though their presence ought to have reassured us, it didn't.

"Take us to a hotel," they demanded.

"This is your hotel," the driver insisted.

Giselle and I looked at each other. "Do you think we've been kidnapped?" we whispered after reaching the privacy of our bedroom. We stayed up most of the night, worrying.

---

* **The oud is an Arabic lute, shaped like a guitar but rounder, thicker, and resonating in much deeper sounds. The Mid-Eastern oud is the lute from which all European lutes were born.**

*They pursed their lips and said
"You musn't wander around." I
wondered how a person was
supposed to explore a   **3**
foreign country if not
allowed to venture outside.*

Upon awakening, I listened for sounds that might inform me
as to our situation. The Spanish conversation of a family in
the house next door filtered through my wall. Surely this
could not be a hotel—I could detect not a trace of hustle or
bustle on streets outside, and our room was like a small
apartment, with a private sitting room, a bedroom with two
beds, and a bathroom.

A chorus of odd new sounds filtered through the door:
gurgling and goo-goos and enchanting little chirps—"Dahh?"
A house that tinkled with such tiny voices seemed decidedly
unsinister, so Giselle and I slipped out of our private suite to
find a salon full of American and European couples holding
babies; bright-colored plastic toys and baby paraphernalia
were scattered everywhere. Our new musicians, Isa and
Karim, looked grouchy.

"Cafe?"

The head maid, Nina, was a cheerful woman whose
twinkling brown eyes didn't let a scrap of information escape
them. She smiled reassuringly.

"Okay," we ventured.

Nina brought out delicious croissants and warm fragrant
bread, heavy silver pots of dark coffee and little carafes filled

with steamed milk, all heaped and balanced on a decorative wicker tray.

While savoring what I hoped was not my last breakfast, I suggested stepping out to see Bogotá. "Colombia is very dangerous," they clucked. They were American women; smiling, thoroughly content, patting their babies and pursing their lips. "You musn't wander around."

I struggled to replace the heavy silver pot on the uneven wicker tray that Nina handled so easily, wondering how a person was supposed to explore a foreign country if not allowed to venture outside. "Is this a hotel?" I asked.

"Oh no. Mr. Zeytun decided you should stay in a *residencia*," Nina replied. In Colombia, upscale boarding houses are called *residencias* (not to be confused with another kind of *residencia*, which lively twosomes rent by the hour). "This *residencia* caters to foreign couples adopting children."

My china cup clinked its saucer in appreciation of Colombia's rich, steaming coffee. "So you are adopting this baby," I said to an American woman. "How cute!" I put my pinky finger into a tiny brown hand for a squeeze.

Karim grimaced, looking like a frog that had hopped into a puddle of piddle. Clearly, he didn't see the point of having babies around; he was a violinist of some importance (at least to himself), and besides, he was the leader of the group, and the one in charge of money matters. He felt his opinions should be taken seriously.

We ignored him. "People come to Colombia from all over the world to adopt infants," said Nina. She smoothed her prim blue uniform, with its little white buttons marching up the front.

Something about Nina made me feel that I could ask her anything. Though she looked to be in her forties and surrounded us in maternal warmth, she was still quite slender. Taller than most Colombian women, she had perhaps been rather striking in her youth. Her thick black hair was carefully styled into a classic above-the-shoulders wave.

"Why do they come all the way to Colombia to adopt children?" I asked.

"Colombia has many children available for adoption. They are born of unwed mothers, or of families too poor to feed them. Our government handles all the adoptive placements, because it is illegal for private agencies to do adoption."

"An agency back in our country helps set everything up," added a European woman. "Both parents must interview personally with the *Instituto de Bienestar Familiar* and after that, one parent must stay in Colombia for about a month while the court approves the adoption."

Giselle, Abe and I each decided immediately that we adored living in a sprawling *residencia* filled with adoptive families. Isa and Karim complained nonstop.

4

*It is this almost dizzying
sense of walking through
history, of touching and
smelling unusual things,
that makes one yearn to
wander the globe.*

I had hoped to immerse myself in at least a bit of Bogotá
while traveling to and from work, but between the bustling
shopping street that held the restaurant and the *residencia* lay
only manicured embassies and carefully guarded blocks of
wealthy homes. Every day, at first, we did as we were told: no
wandering, just meek commuting from the *residencia* to the
"Libano Restaurant," where we danced seven lunches and six
dinners a week.

An opportunity to sight-see finally arrived on Sunday
afternoon when Mr. Zeytun, the owner of the Libano restaurant, took us on an excursion. He drove one car and his 80-
year-old father drove another. Riding with Grandpa Zeytun,
we climbed high into the mountains, zipping along winding
and potholed roads dodging pigs, chickens, donkey carts,
bicycles, dogs, motorcycles, cows, pedestrians and the occasional speeding car.

I expected to experience that uniquely delicious sense of
displacement reserved for sight-seeing tourists, but this felt
instead ... almost like a homecoming. An oddly familiar
sensation had tugged at me several times during my first few
days in Bogotá. The houses, and even the maids, felt as if

I had known them before. Sometimes, I could even predict the outcome of random conversations, as if I'd dreamt those words and could still glimpse them, deep in my subconscious being.

I pushed these peculiar feelings aside, but as we rose higher and higher into the mountains, feelings of familiarity became impossible to ignore. Perhaps this was reminding me of my early childhood in the Rocky Mountains. The air was crisp and cold and the pine-forested mountains resembled those in Colorado.

We stopped along the roadside to eat colossal ears of corn, roasted in the husk over charcoal grills; then again for sweet strawberries with cream; we bought fresh cheese from farmers, and ate *arepas* (flavorless cornmeal patties). We would have basked in the pleasures of sight-seeing—that is, if it was to be survived.

Grandpa Zeytun obviously needed new bifocals, and if he were in America, his license would be permanently revoked. We teetered over cliffs, confronted cows face-to-face, and honked profusely, demanding that everyone clear the way for grandpa's hurried ascent.

Abe screamed in Arabic and hid his head as we bounced through the forest, narrowly missing an oncoming truck. At one point we heard a loud thump and a dog limped away. "*Malesh*," said Grandpa Zeytun as he sped on. "No big deal," in Arabic.

Returning to Bogotá, I reassessed Colombia's dangers. The people seemed harmless, especially compared to many neighbors I've had in Miami. I vowed to go anywhere, do anything, but be very careful crossing the street and check the sidewalks for wayward vehicles.

The next afternoon I tested my newfound independence by walking to the local shopping mall. It was an uneventful journey, but I liked discovering things for myself so I boarded a bus to "Chapinero," a lively shopping area full of street vendors and cheap stores.

The air in Bogotá was laden with a distinctive gasoline smell; not the sick-sweet scent that lingers on your hands when you are too sloppy at the self-serve, but a burning smell, of cars combusting their fuel. It was unhealthily leaded, but I found myself growing fond of it.

More confident after wandering Chapinero, I headed downtown in search of "La Candelaria." I couldn't find it, but downtown was a lively, bustling place that reminded me of parts of Brooklyn. I did all my Christmas shopping.

It seemed like an unequal struggle, this Bogotánian traffic: countrified folk trundled right down busy streets in ancient horse-drawn carts while slick, speeding Mercedes tried to out-muscle gasping and wheezing clunker taxis; now and then a small burro pulled his load amidst all the honking and jostling.

At precisely 5 p.m., soldiers started flipping rifles and

marching. An enthusiastic band played the Colombian national anthem. They also played irresistible *cumbia* and *salsa* tunes that made a whole plaza full of people feel like dancing, and put smiles on the faces of stern soldiers, who flirted and waved and escorted young ladies across the street. This was the changing of the guard at the president's palace, full of pomp and circumstance and sizzle.

And then it happened again: some deep and dormant memory, triggered this time by the *cumbia* rhythm, provoking sudden and intense emotions that I could not interpret. Even the Colombian national anthem—played by a band that was not always on key—produced an inexplicable feeling of pride.

People fed pigeons, folk groups danced and political proselytizers aired their views. I went back many times. When students staged demonstrations, soldiers with automatic weapons lined the plaza on all sides. Seldom did people hear the voice of Colombia's machine guns, and until later, when I stumbled into a conversation with a guerrilla revolutionary after traveling back roads on a bus, all the guns just seemed like window dressing, adding a touch of drama to a strangely familiar foreign country. When there were no demonstrations, a kaleidoscope of musicians and dancers performed in the plaza.

Then I found La Candelaria. It is an area of narrow, hilly cobblestone streets and whitewashed 17th century Spanish buildings, many wearing plaques telling their stories. In this historic place, it was not hard to picture the last 500 years.

Before the Spanish arrived in present-day Colombia in 1499, the area where Bogotá now sits was populated by Muisca Indians. They were displaced by conquistadors, who thought and acted like ruthless entrepreneurs and had just one goal in mind: to line their pockets with gold. The conquistadors used Bogotá as a base for expeditions into Colombia's mountainous interior.

The buildings in La Candelaria were built mainly by a different group of Spaniards, the administrators, who had a goal they considered more noble: to obtain wealth for the crown. A third group of Spaniards, the Roman Catholic clergy, built churches all over Colombia. Their mission was to save native Indian souls (and, while saving the Indians, to acquire Indian land for the church).

It is this almost dizzying sense of walking through history, of touching and smelling unusual things, that makes one yearn to wander the globe. I stretched, feeling immensely lucky to be here, realizing that I had underestimated the power of Kaaren's advice. Indeed, trading that caseworker job for a career as a traveling dancer had been the most important decision of my life. Like many artists, I had no real prospects for monetary wealth, but I reveled in the luxury of dancing, all expenses paid, in Bogotá, where I could scrunch along the sidewalk of La Candelaria, zoom through mountains chasing sun-baked curves, and return home to maids and a private suite in a spacious white stucco *residencia*.

*As an American, I was
expected to befriend only
the "upper class" —
regardless of how they
made their money*

5

Back in the Libano Restaurant, I came to know the regular
customers. A fleshy Lebanese man named Khasif came in often,
accompanied by six bodyguards. I noticed that some of his
bodyguards stayed by his car, others stood in the entry of the
restaurant, and two sat by him at the table; every one of the
guards said they came from a mysterious place called the
Guajira Peninsula. They never let go of the briefcases under
their arms.

One day, Khasif invited us on an outing to his textile
factory. Giselle, Abe and I rode in a white chauffeur-driven
Mercedes while Karim and Isa followed in a shaky Renault.
Each car carried its own guard. I wondered why our body-
guard kept his briefcase pointed out the window with his
finger near the latch, until he showed me that his briefcase, at
the touch of a button, became a machine gun.

We toured Khasif's warehouse, his friend's blue jean
factory, and an underwear factory. Though the factories
contained rows of sewing machines and scores of employees,
Khasif's warehouses seemed to contain sparse quantities of
merchandise. Khasif soon distracted such thinking by procur-
ing generous gifts for us everywhere we went, sending us
home with armloads of complimentary fabrics, jeans, T-shirts

and underwear, but I couldn't help wondering why his thinly stocked textile warehouse required six bodyguards with machine guns. When somebody in Colombia is rich, nobody questions why.

Regardless of how they made their money, people like Khasif were held in high esteem by everyone around me. It was Khasif's popularity, and the expectation that I should consort with such people, that formed my introduction to Colombia's intransigent class system, a tradition of injustice in Colombia that seems to rival (or even exceed) the USA's problems with racism.

In Colombia, American entertainers like me were supposed to conform to a kind of movie-star fantasy; perfect cupie doll features or, better yet, blue eyes and blonde hair. My bosses wanted American entertainers to look like the ones on television. I couldn't help them with that—somewhere along the line my English-German-French heritage assembled itself into a distinctively ethnic look, so much so that when I seek costume supplies in Mid-Eastern import shops customers ask me to wait on them, assuming I am Turkish or Egyptian; in Latin America most people thought I was a local.

The Hollywood illusion was also supposed to include befriending the right class of people. As an American entertainer, I was not supposed to spend my time with people considered beneath me—which was nearly everyone I wanted to hang out with. Giselle and Abe were nice, but 20 years older than I was, and they worried about danger and preferred not to go out around town; Isa and Karim were interested only in drinking and locating the nearest supply of prostitutes; and Khasif's generous gifts did nothing to motivate me to spend time with him or his shady friends. I preferred more down-to-earth folks who were closer to my own age; people who shared my interests. People like Delio.

They told me it was unseemly to befriend the likes of Delio, the doorman at the Libano. Delio was 18 years old with a 15-year-old's face; he had jet black hair, a cinnamon suntan, and was one of the few people I met who was willing to reach out to homeless kids (who, I later learned, were considered the ultimate in unseemly friendships). Okay, so Delio was not a member of my assigned class—we enjoyed each other's company and liked to take little jaunts around town together.

"Have you been to Monserrate?" he asked one day, as we wandered along near downtown Bogotá.

"What is it?"

"It's up the mountain—you take a skyride to get to it."

"Up the mountain? Of course I want to go!"

I thought for a moment. "What's up there, anyway?"

"Monserrate. It's a church."

"Oh."

"But not just a church. Monserrate is known for miracles,"

he said, "it is famous all over Colombia."

As we sat in the comfort of the *teleferico* (skyride), gliding uphill, we looked down at villagers climbing the mountainside on foot. "What's that guy doing?" I asked, studying a fellow who was scuffing up the mountain on his knees.

"People make pilgrimages, hiking up the mountain to pay homage. The most pious, like him, even hike up on their knees," said Delio. "We're almost there. When we get to the village we'll buy candles."

"How much?" I asked, knowing that Delio had little money.

"Only one *peso*."

We stepped off the skyride into a little village of touristy shops and stalls, with knick-knacks and doo-dads and tiny toilets on keychains. Surrounding the white church of Monserrate were photos and crutches, left to express gratitude for Monserrate's healing miracles.

Placing our flickering candles into years of accumulated wax drippings, we walked through the dimly lit sanctuary, taking care not to disturb the meditations of an old woman dressed in peasant clothes and a woolen shawl. There were rarely many people in there. It was always very dark, its gold glimmering quietly in the shadows. And every time I set foot in the ancient church, a feeling of peace settled upon me.

On the way back, Delio and I stopped in a leather shop where I admired various things and was particularly intrigued

by a belt. Unbeknownst to me, Delio had made an arrange-
ment with the owner. "See what she wants and I'll buy it for
her," he told the man. Although we had developed a congenial
friendship, Delio's gift came as a surprise; he earned less than
one-twentieth of my salary. I was touched by his generosity.

On another outing, we happened upon an emerald store.
Hundreds of glittering emeralds winked us into the shop,
where a Colombian salesman approached instantly.

"What kind of jewelry are you seeking?" he asked,
affecting a painstaking British accent.

"Um, just checking out the emeralds."

"What grade are you looking for?"

Delio and I looked at each other and shrugged. The
salesman pulled out drawer after drawer of sparkling green
stones, thousands of emeralds in all sizes, shapes and shades
of green. Colombia, I discovered, produces 90 percent of the
world's emeralds. Watching the salesman with his magnifying
glass and pair of tweezers, I fantasized about using these little
piles of emeralds to bead a costume.

6

Fending off Karim became as much a part of my nightly routine as donning veils of silk.

Twice, we almost got evicted from the *residencia* because of Karim and Isa, our sullen middle aged adolescents. Before leaving the restaurant where we worked, they would guzzle down whiskey. Then, reeking of booze, Karim would sneak into the kitchen and steal several bottles to get him through the night.

After Nina retired to the maid's quarters to sleep, Jaime (the Libano's 19-year-old manager) started delivering prostitutes to the *residencia*. The two musicians would tiptoe to the foyer like kids checking their Christmas stockings, let them in, then sneak back to their rooms for bawdy bedroom parties. Or so the babies informed us—all the carousing woke them up, and they sounded an alarm that resembled a chorus of cats, alerting everyone in the house. The owner of the *residencia* was furious!

"Please, let them stay," pleaded Mr. Zeytun. "There will be no more trouble."

"This is a place for families!"

"I know, I know. It will not happen again."

The *residencia's* owner remained unconvinced.

Then our boss got a brainstorm. "Here, you see? Nina will

handle it!" announced Mr. Zeytun. The two men clapped each other on the back, the matter resolved.

Controlling Isa and Karim seemed like a daunting proposition to me, but Nina smiled, as always, and appeared quite poised. She gazed placidly at the front door, like a lioness assessing a new den for an especially non-compliant set of cubs.

"What will you do?" I asked.

"*Tengo un plan*," she said cheerfully. ("I have come up with a plan.")

Later that day, she called Giselle and I to the door.

"You see? I am locking the door with this key. Those mischief-makers won't be able to open the door tonight, even from the inside!" With a wink, Nina went to bed. Still wide awake after our evening performance, we hid in the kitchen.

Tap, tap, tap.

Giselle elbowed me as Karim jiggled the handle, muttering to himself. While Giselle and I tried to muffle our giggles, Karim launched a volley of violent and desperate attacks on the new lock, but he could not open the door to let in his friends-for-hire. Apparently they didn't want his company as badly as he wanted theirs, because they soon left to find more accessible companions.

Karim's libido continued to search out every available female. Though he dressed decently and wasn't fat, his shape wasn't good and he smelled like liquor. Even if a woman could be attracted to his marshmallowy body, she would have to contend with a repellant personality. He'd sit around making rude comments in Arabic about women who walked by, discussing every intimate feature of their faces and bodies.

After appointing himself to handle the money, he tried to cheat us on our pay. Following a particularly contentious week when Abe, Giselle and I all fought with him about the money he owed us, Karim decided—without asking my opinion—that I should be his girlfriend. Fending him off soon became as much a part of my nightly routine as putting on makeup and donning veils of silk.

"Let's get together tonight."

I pushed him away. "It's time for the show."

"Stick with me and you won't have to dance anymore."

"Why would I want to quit dancing?"

"For me."

"How excruciating. It's time for you to go on, Karim."

He didn't budge. "You're frigid, that's your problem. I think you're a lesbian."

He began to pick at what he perceived to be my faults until finally I released my pent-up frustration by planting a foot on his pants and kicking as hard as I possibly could, sending him flying onto the stage, violin in hand. When Karim recovered his wits and started his music, I danced out with a snarl on my face. The audience froze, stunned, until they deduced Karim's rejection. Then guffaws and gusts of applause, like buckets of confetti, erupted out of the audience.

7

*Patrons pulled pistols out
of their belts and plopped
them on the table.
Mr. Zeytun said their
wealth made them targets.*

By then, we had become acclimated to the thin atmosphere.
Bogotá is perched at an 8,600 foot (2,600 meter) elevation,
and the first few shows felt like dancing up a thousand flights
of stairs. Even the musicians became exhausted.

We danced in bare feet, improvising our choreography to
work through four luxurious mirrored dining rooms, maneuvering around lots of plants and a luscious Lebanese buffet.
Stinging distractions—tiny droplets of sweat, produced by
skylights and spotlighting—spilled into our eyes as we tried to
maintain pleasant expressions.

If you dance with the veil in confined spaces it wants to
catch on the chandeliers or touch people's food, yet the allure
of floating silk was such that I danced with it anyway. Taking
care to avoid terrestrial challenges, I would start my performance with my veils folded like angel wings; lifting with the
music, the fabric floated up around my shoulders to wrap me
in a silk cocoon; momentarily, my veil would become a
turban, and sometimes, with a little sleight of hand, I hid
myself completely.

And then I would gild my choreography with a sword,
balancing it on my head while performing hip figure-eights,

or suspending it on an extended hip as I did intricate isolation movements. Images of immovable swords on an undulating dancer never failed to entrance the audience.

We tried to synchronize our movements to the musicians, but Karim was a stage hog and had a tendency to interrupt our dancing to play egotistical violin solos. Oblivious to the local audience's desire for a full palette of lively music, Karim chose to smother them with *taqsims*, which are unstructured arhythmic improvisations not easily appreciated by untrained ears. Even if the audience had been composed entirely of ethnic violin connoisseurs, I suspect that Karim's intrusive (and lengthy) solos would have been received as lectures rather than entertainment.

The Libano catered to a rich clientele. They seldom tipped the dancers, although a young Cuban sugar-grower once tipped me with a US $100 bill. Most people simply watched while they ate their dinners.

Women in custom-designed wool suits, or outfits made of leather from head to toe, encouraged us to get their men up to dance, so their conservative-looking guys in dark suits could look like fools for just a moment and they could laugh and snap photos. But the men were shy. And the women made fun of them. So husbands, fathers and brothers had to get a little alcohol in their systems. When a man gained enough confidence to dance, I would guide him through a few movements with my veil around his hips, and others would beg me to dance with *their* men.

I would have preferred to showcase Mid-Eastern dance as an art form instead of circulating between tables encouraging men to be ridiculed, but such artistic idealism would not have been welcomed, so I catered to local preferences. Colombia was an adventure worth that particular price.

Thank goodness I didn't have to endure what happened to Giselle. I'm sure I wouldn't have handled it as graciously. Many men drank incredible amounts of Colombia's anise-flavored *aguardiente* (sugarcane liquor, literally, "burning water"). One night, a big snockered man jumped up and hoisted Giselle into his arms, stumbling right onto the open stage in front of the musicians. He swung her around and around, ignoring her screams as she begged him to let her go, finally falling flat and passing out—right on top of her. Giselle just slinked out from underneath him and continued the show, demonstrating her class and professionalism. But it disgusted me, this fat slob who thought he could disrespect a sophisticated middle-aged woman and then fall down drunk, without even getting thrown out of the restaurant!

Such besotted foolishness, however, was not typical; usually drunken Colombians didn't get loud and boisterous like American men. The more they drank, the more quietly they sat, until finally they put their heads on the table and went to sleep.

Clang!

They are tiny, carved delicately in silver, and they hide discreetly in my palms when I want them to. But finger cymbals produce a dramatic noise—surprisingly loud—when you play them just right. As I danced by konked-out men I clashed my finger cymbals in their ears. Sometimes they startled. Sometimes they didn't.

The first time a group of patrons pulled pistols out of their belts and plopped them on the table, I kept my distance. "What's with the guns?" I asked Mr. Zeytun.

"It is not comfortable to have a gun in your waistband while you feast on my buffet," he said.

"Well—why do they need guns?"

He stroked his thick mustache. "Wealth is always a target," he said. "They feel more secure when they carry weapons."

Throughout the evening those menacing *pistolas* would remain on dinner tables, "protecting" their owners. Still, it seemed to me that if *I* didn't need a gun to protect myself, these big macho types flashing their guns must have been rather weak characters. Their heavy drinking was also less than captivating.

"Don't you think it's unsafe to have people drinking with guns sitting on the table?"

Mr. Zeytun shrugged.

As men snored on gun-festooned tables, I danced right on by, keeping my finger cymbals to myself.

When you dance, you bare your soul to the audience. When you dance for people who are too drunk to appreciate it, or for people you can't respect, it feels like a compromise. However, one place offered me an audience who expected no concessions, inviting me to express myself exactly as I liked.

My favorite Colombian venue was called *Media Torta* (Half a Cake). Every foreign entertainer who performs in Bogotá must do a show at *Media Torta*, an outdoor theatre that shivers high on the side of a mountain. Here the government sponsors a nationally televised variety show every Sunday. Because admission is free, Colombia's poverty-stricken masses pour in by the hundreds. This warm and responsive audience more than compensated for frigid conditions, showering us with fan letters, offering pictures of our show drawn on scraps of paper, and always, giving us free rein to perform straight from the heart.

*We call them "gamines."
Many, like Oscar, have
nowhere to sleep but the
street ... no families will
take them in.*

8

Oscar

After midnight, when the restaurant closed, we used to walk
the dim streets back to our *residencia*, treading cautiously on
dark sidewalks whose missing tiles formed toe-stubbers for
the unwary. A small tin cart on four big wheels, its faded red
and yellow paint glimmering dull gray in the moonlight,
reposed on the corner. Hand-painted on the side of the wagon,
a sign advertised, "Hot Dogs."

Behind the cart, a cardboard box—large enough to cover a
bicycle—began to move. Suddenly the top popped off, just
long enough to reveal a pair of boy-sized eyes, the brightest
spots in a smudged little face.

"Hello there. Is this where you live?"

He turned away. I had seen many children roaming the
streets, begging for food or money, sometimes stealing a bit or
a trinket before dashing into an alley. But visiting a street
child at home was new.

"What's your name?"

He didn't answer. Wrapped in an old sweater and holding
a broken bottle, he slid deeper into his cardboard sleeping

box. It was November—summer in Colombia, but the altitude was high and the nights were cold.

I knew who he was. I had seen this uncombed little urchin often. He rarely spoke, except to mumble shy requests for *pesos*, and he used pieces of broken glass to defend himself from the other street children, who ran in gangs. Every day I spoke to him as I passed by, eventually learning that his name was Oscar.

"Oscar, tell me about yourself," I said.

He took his time answering. "*Yo vengo de Villavicencio*," he said finally. "I come from Villavicencio." It was a small town southeast of Bogotá.

"Do you have a family?" I asked.

He shrugged. I let the silence guide us, and eventually he explained. "My sister. Her husband is cruel."

"What does he do that's cruel?"

"He used to beat me." He looked up at me in brown-eyed defiance. "So I live here now."

I didn't want to ask questions that would upset him, but I had to know. "What about your parents?"

"My mother, my father, my baby brother, they died," his small, husky voice told me. "on *La Noche Buena* (Christmas Eve). They drank tainted milk."

"But there are places that take in children who have no families. Maybe we can find one."

"No. I've been there." He averted his dark eyes. "I hate

Dallal

them," he said hoarsely.

I later found out that many of Colombia's orphanages have nasty reputations for child abuse. Every time a social worker took Oscar to one of Bogotá's strict orphanages, he escaped.

I asked Nina why so many children suffered alone on the streets.

"We call them *gamines*," she said. "Some live with their families, but must beg or sell trinkets to earn enough money to fill their empty stomachs. But many others, like Oscar, have nowhere to sleep but the street. No families will take them in." Nina never hesitated to speak her mind, expressing clearly defined views in the gentlest of voices. "You see, the government controls our adoption system, and they want parents to have money. But affluent Colombian families will never adopt a child of a lower class. Colombia has a big problem with homeless children."

Another little *gamin* explained: "I live on the street because my family has too many children and too little to eat."

"Do your brothers and sisters live at home?" I asked.

"Yes. Because I am oldest, I was chosen to go out on my own." He was ten.

Oscar didn't know how to read or write, so I bought a notebook and pencils and set up our classroom on the sidewalk. Wealthy shoppers stopped and stared at the American girl sitting on the curb, teaching an orphan that society had abandoned. They were generous with nosy stares, though not with pesos for Oscar. It was with pesos that Oscar had taught himself to add and subtract. Since math seemed to come easily to him, I showed him how to write numbers and use plus and minus signs. A few hours later, Oscar was solving arithmetic problems with pencil and paper.

When we found it difficult to brush away distractions on the busy sidewalk, the local pizza parlor offered us a table for our lessons. Here we found a special kindness, as they gave us free sodas and helped Oscar find a safe place to keep his sweater and piece of cardboard, letting him eat while he studied. Soon he could write his name and mine, as well as a few favorite words.

My teaching did not go unpaid. The sour expression Oscar had worn on his cute little wind-chapped face disappeared, replaced by smiles and mischievous eyes as he made presents for me out of napkins and paper cups, each day opening up just a little more, letting me know a friendly little boy who loved practical jokes. Perhaps affection had become plausible for him again, after so much time growing up alone.

I noticed that Oscar's belly bulged. At first I thought he was fat, but then he showed me his stash: extra clothes and small boy treasures that he kept under his decrepit sweater.

I felt a need to see Oscar stuff at least one more treasure

into the thicket of trinkets under his sweater, so I bought him a small wooden ball attached to a stick with a string, a toy that is popular with Colombian children. Almost immediately, another street child tried to steal Oscar's new toy. Stockier than his attacker, though poorly fed, Oscar held his own with the help of his broken bottle, and assured me that I shouldn't worry, as he usually wins these contests. (But he didn't. Three other children succeeded in stealing his present the very next day.)

All children deserve to be tucked in when they go to bed, so every night after my performance I stopped by to kiss Oscar good night. Sometimes when I arrived after work he would pretend to be asleep, but he could not hold back giggles when I approached. Other times he was missing. Just as I would start to wonder if some unexpected menace had befallen my young friend, out Oscar would pounce, making some funny little noise that he perceived to be terrifying.

One night something happened that really did scare me. When I came to give him a hug, Oscar was nowhere to be found. When one of your favorite friends is missing, you go to their home—but Oscar had no home. You call their friends—but the few people who had befriended Oscar had no telephones, and it was after midnight. So you check their favorite haunts, and if you still can't find your friend, you worry.

The following day, very worried, I asked the hot dog

vendor if he knew what had happened to Oscar. I knew that if Oscar was okay he would turn up at the hot dog cart. The cart's owner, having grown up as a street child himself, had given Oscar the job of guarding the cart overnight, and paid wages that seemed pretty fair for a street kid: one free hot dog each morning. Sure enough, the hot dog vendor had an answer for me. He told me the police had taken Oscar to a juvenile detention center, saying they would keep him there until an orphanage was found for him.

At first, I figured it was for the best, for children belong in safe places, and what place could be safer than a home for children? But nasty little concerns crept into dark places in my mind. I prayed that reports of abuse I'd heard were untrue. I hoped the hot dog man told me the truth, that nothing worse had happened to Oscar. I tried to figure out a way to reach my little friend. I felt impotent, until my worries, shimmering like heat waves on a dry afternoon, suddenly lifted and disappeared. Oscar had escaped and come back. This time.

With all the foreigners wanting to adopt children, I hoped that maybe someone might want to take in this lovable round-faced 13-year-old, stunted from malnutrition, who looked and acted 10. I took Oscar to the agency that helped people at my *residencia* adopt their children. "Wait here," said a business-like woman in a dowdy green dress.

We waited around and eventually she returned with a pile of documents. "Fill these out now, please." Wondering how street kids who didn't have interested adults to read and write for them could ever make their way onto Colombian adoption lists, I handed the social worker a set of completed documents, and she began to question Oscar.

"Haven't you run away from orphanages before?" Evidently wiser than me, or more jaded, he didn't bother to tell her that paying for a roof over one's head by accepting beatings isn't much of a bargain. He just said nothing.

"Why should we send you to a family? You will only run away again."

"No, no, I won't. I would stay with a family, please."

The social worker told me to take him to a reformatory, and suggested one that was infamous for its brutality.

In his tattered wool sweater and incredibly dirty jeans (street children lack bathtubs and can't squander *pesos* on laundry), Oscar needed a way to clean up, so I invited him to the *residencia* to use our shower. After dissolving many layers of dirt, we went to the living room for conversation and made Christmas decorations from colored paper.

"Nina, could you bring some hot chocolate for me and my little friend?" I asked. Nina prepared pots of her wonderful hot chocolate for me every day, to energize me and help me maintain enough curves to fill my costumes. My performance schedule—four 45-minute shows every day—was so intense that, without Nina's rich chocolate drink, I tended to drop weight drastically.

"Nina?"

No response.

She didn't refuse to make the chocolate. She just seemed not to hear me. Though Nina had a never-ending supply of smiles for the babies in the *residencia*, she frowned at my little friend. Her silence quarantined Oscar into that place Colombian society has reserved for its unwanted citizens. I made the chocolate myself.

Nina later told me her boss wouldn't allow Oscar in the *residencia*, despite its focus on a clientele who adopted orphans. *Okay*, I thought, *so I'll adopt an orphan myself*. I had saved $700. Nina showed me the ropes and I began the formalities of international adoption.

"You cannot," officials told me. "You do not have the money."

"I have $700."

"You are not qualified."

"What are the qualifications?"

"You have no husband."

"I heard that single people can adopt older orphans," I countered.

"You own no property."

"I can provide more shelter than his piece of cardboard."

"You are too young."

"I'll offer him more protection than a broken bottle—I've seen people attack him!"

"We cannot allow it."

Perhaps I'm missing something, but isn't there something fundamentally wrong with letting a child live in a corrugated box when an adult wants to take responsibility for him?

I continued to pester people, but discovered that I needed to come up with $800 just for the lawyer. There were other expenses—medical exams, immigration papers, fingerprinting and court fees, not to mention plane tickets and a passport for Oscar. Colombian adoption fees were approximately US $3,800—not including foster care, travel, or local agency fees. My $700 was not nearly enough and even if it was, they would not have allowed me to adopt him.

"Please," I asked officials, "can't you find some way to give Oscar a home?"

The social worker sighed. "Here's an address," she said, pressing a scrap of paper into my hand. "I promise you it is a lovely orphanage."

Oscar and I conferred, and he agreed to give it a chance. Our huge hand-painted taxi, circa 1950s, belched, popped and puffed black smoke as it took us to what I hoped would be Oscar's new home. When we arrived at a dingy building that looked like a dreadfully depressing school, Oscar refused to get out of the taxi.

"I know this place," he pleaded, "It won't work." His eyes

spoke eloquently, but it was my last hope.

"Come with me. It won't be so bad." I took his hand and held it tightly as we walked in.

The pickle-faced woman in the office recognized Oscar. "You?" she snapped. "This is for orphans, not delinquents. Get him out of here!" She pointed angrily at the door.

It was a hateful place and, stung by such blatant rejection, Oscar started to cry. I cried. Even the driver cried. We slumped into the seat of the cab. As I blinked away tears, I watched Oscar, realizing that all options were exhausted, wondering if he knew.

Society's cold shoulders can be so broad, so invincible, so padded with indifference that they seem more like walls than human features. Determined not to let our bruises end our friendship, I resolved to show Oscar as much fun as possible. We continued our pizza-parlor schooling and went on outings to the circus and movies. Meals in a restaurant were a new joy for Oscar, though some of the owners were not happy to serve a little *gamin*—yet they didn't mind when people brought dogs into the restaurant.

It occurred to me, seeing such differences in access to power (not to mention basic amenities), that Colombia was like Europe in the Middle Ages. You were born into a certain position in society and you would never be able to change it. People were not equal, and everything about you showed your social standing—your movements, your way of talking, your clothes, your body language, the expression on your face. Oscar was Superglued into a position without privileges.

I could not stay in Colombia without a visa; I could not have a visa without a dance assignment; my dance assignment was for only a month; I could not bring Oscar back to Miami without an adoption. When I explained this to Oscar, he did not react one way or another, resigned to his lot in life, as if he knew I was wasting my time from the beginning. Though he probably didn't understand my dilemma, he never seemed to hold any illusions about anyone actually taking him in.

The last days before I left, Oscar avoided all talk about my departure, and even more disconcerting, slept on another corner so I couldn't find him. The night before leaving, I found Oscar in his open-air bedroom near the hot dog cart, sleeping in his cardboard box huddled in his blanket, broken bottle by his side.

Bidding a friend farewell is hard enough, but lifting the only piece of cardboard that shields a child from the cold to tell him good-bye is heartbreaking. When I kissed Oscar good night he wouldn't open his eyes, no matter what I did. Silent resignation. No hugs, no good-byes. It was a horrible way to leave.

I never saw Oscar again. When I returned to Bogotá five months later, I walked the streets with a heart full of hope, looking for a stocky boy with a lively face and worn out clothes. I asked the street children about him, but no one knew anything about the boy with a sweater full of treasures who used to guard the hot dog stand.

Conditions for gamines have worsened since the 1980s.

Human rights organizations claim that vigilante groups are now executing gamines in a so-called "social cleansing" effort, dumping bodies into clandestine cemeteries.

Other gamines die in an even grislier scheme: Colombian traffickers have been accused of killing street children to sell body organs.

Of 2,190 known child murders in Colombia during 1993, only 12 were ever brought to trial.

My heart sank. Four weeks in Bogotá had not allowed me to know Colombia at all.

9

Return to Miami

The roof of the *Aeropuerto Eldorado* was lined with a double quota of soldiers clutching assault weapons—hundreds of serious young boys were stitched together shoulder to shoulder to form a security wall that couldn't spare the width of a grin. Someone told us the president was coming.

It seemed a dramatic ending for my trip, just like in the movies, except that it wasn't about me.

President Betancur had been elected a year before I arrived and was beset with problems. Drug barons were laundering cash so enthusiastically that fundamental market forces got skewed, causing real estate and construction investments to bloat into uncontrollable inflation.

He had been trying to pacify guerrilla groups, who were puffing like squashed sponges following removal of a particularly repressive state of siege. Aiming for a truce, Betancur chose to experiment with new guerrilla-friendly policies that didn't do a thing to disarm guerrillas, but did make both drug lords and his own army very nervous. His new policies especially upset Colombia's drug Mafiosos, who wanted disarmed guerrillas or none at all. Guerrilla "fund raising"

What exactly is a "state of siege?"

Colombia's National Security Statute allows the president to set aside civil rights when he declares a state of siege. Here's what happens:
1. The government censors the media.
2. Military police are authorized to search and seize any person, for any reason.
3. Military tribunals get to prosecute crimes

(kidnapping and extortion) targeted their wealth.

I didn't fully understand Betancur's can of worms and wondered what all the fuss was about. At any rate, his new policies survived until my plane departed and I never caught a glimpse of the beleaguered Betancur—I just winged back to the United States wondering what to do next.

Feelings of affinity for Colombia were so penetrating that I could not accept my departure. My heart sank; four weeks in Bogotá had not allowed me to know Colombia at all. What would happen to Oscar? And those odd feelings of *deja vu*— what caused them? I needed to come back. Surely, I thought, there must be a way to dance back across this border.

I won't say the five months back in Miami were uneventful—home can be about as adventurous as travel, provided you don't spend all your time in a carefully manicured suburb. A geekoid Saudi prince kidnapped me (I attributed it to an unusually lame attempt to get a date) and in an unrelated incident, I arrived to dance at a wedding only to discover a

Dallal

strange ceremony with a woman trying to marry the devil.

I came home from an evening of belly dancing at birthday parties to find a message from Mr. Zeytun on my answering machine. "I want you to come back to dance for the Libano," he said, "bring two more dancers—they must be beautiful— one blonde and one brunette."

Wanting to wow the folks in Colombia, I rounded up Azuri and La Donn, two gorgeous dancers recommended by the Club Ibis in New York, women of outstanding talent with 10 years' more experience than me.

The "contract" was for a month, but I planned to stay three months, to explore. I was thinking of traveling by bus, then maybe going to Ecuador and Peru, but when I went to the Colombian tourist bureau in Miami they said no. "It's impossible to go by bus," the travel consultant insisted. "You have to take a tour."

"*Why* is it impossible?" I asked.

"Because it is."

When I pressed for an explanation, I found out it was a class thing. Lower class people take busses; I wasn't considered lower class, therefore it was impossible for me to take a bus. Ignoring the travel consultant's advice, I began to plan an extended trip to off-the-beaten-path places.

Had I known about Mr. Zeytun's habit of double-booking, I might have been more cautious about liquidating everything I own. Mr. Zeytun, it turned out, liked to hire two groups at the same time. One group got tickets—the other got ditched. Although we referred to the job as a contract, there was never any written document to protect us. Most traveling belly dancers work without formal contracts, and most employers in the Arabic community are honorable enough to keep their word.

Three days before leaving, I tried to prepay my rent.

"Hang on to your money," the woman said. "You'll need to move your things out before you leave."

"Why?"

"The whole block has been sold to Hyatt Hotels. They're going to tear it down while you're in South America."

I didn't mind losing my customized apartment—yes, customized, I had hammered mirror tiles into bits and stuck them to the walls to make designs, and hung up batiks and Asian masks all over the place—I could always redecorate. But I dreaded saying good-bye to my pet car, Putt Putt. Nobody wanted him in their yard and I was sure they weren't going to build the Hyatt Regency around my parking space. I put a sign in the window: *Must Sell Now! $300.*"

Putt Putt was a Ford Falcon about my age. I bought him on a street corner when he had no paint, lacquered him up in fire-engine red, put purple pom-poms around the windows and hung a sad-eyed camel from the mirror.

He had a little rust problem. One day Kaaren, the queenly opera singer, fell through the floor. We were headed to an audition as movie extras, dressed to kill, but when Kaaren

Dallal

stood up the floor dropped to the pavement. After that Kaaren said she was afraid to ride in the front seat. I put in carpeting to cover up the unsightly hole and never lost another passenger, but Kaaren noticed a missing door hinge and worried because I had not yet gone through the formalities of getting a driver's license.

So much for reminiscing. It was time to say good-bye to my pet car. A cute scientist who liked to restore antique cars bargained me down to $299 and putt-putted away.

Now that I was ready to head south, completely unfettered, the consulate dragged its feet about issuing my visa and our plane tickets did not arrive.

I called Mr. Zeytun long distance. "What's going on? I can't go to Bogotá without a visa!"

"Don't worry," he said.

"When will we get our plane tickets?"

"Soon."

A drummer I knew was terribly worried. "Mr. Zeytun hired me too, and another dancer," he said. "I haven't gotten my airline ticket, have you?"

Thinking it was odd that Mr. Zeytun would hire another dancer and a musician without mentioning it to me, I began to feel uneasy.

Azuri had two children and managed a dance school. "I've made all my arrangements. What's happening with our tickets?" she asked.

"Oh, I know Mr. Zeytun. We'll get them," I assured her, sounding more confident than I felt. Azuri wasn't happy with the tenuous ticket situation, and La Donn had quit a full-time job for the trip.

Mr. Zeytun's brother lived in nearby Ft. Lauderdale, so I called him. "Yeah, don't worry. It's all taken care of," he said. But his empty reassurances did not produce any tickets.

I tried Mr. Zeytun again. "Did you double-book us? I heard you hired someone else," I said.

"No, no, I didn't," he said. "There must be another restaurant opening in Bogotá."

"Who are our musicians?"

"I don't want any musicians. Last time they gave me too many headaches."

Still hopeful, I finished sewing a fancy red and silver costume and made 12 new cassette music tapes for our shows.

"We're leaving in three days—what should we do about our visas?"

"No problem," said Mr. Zeytun, unruffled.

Azuri and I received plane tickets the day before the flight. La Donn showed up at the airport three hours before departure without a ticket—it arrived in time, but we never did get our visas. And the other group Mr. Zeytun had strung along was out of luck altogether.

*The glamorous Americans
didn't care to visit
questionable neighborhoods.
I ended up hanging* **10**
*around
with the locals.*

In Bogotá, Colombian bureaucracy was reinventing itself yet again. We piled into a governmentally-gray office and sat down.

"Ah! You see? You need an 'Artistic Visa!'" the man said.

"What is that? I was here five months ago and didn't need one. Why do we need it now?"

"Yes, you all need Artistic Visas," he said, pleased with himself for enforcing the very latest regulations.

"How do we get one?"

"Let me see ... the American police must give you clearance," he said.

"Here it is," I said, selecting a folder from a bundle of documents we had brought along just in case.

"But you need to be examined by a doctor."

"Now?"

"No. Have a doctor in the United States certify that you are disease-free."

"We had checkups. Here's proof."

As I patiently pulled out document after document, Mr. Zeytun discussed our situation with his connections—or made payoffs—and our visas appeared at last.

Azuri and La Donn were super-glamorous, not a flaw on their bodies or anywhere else. Much of their conversation centered on makeup and clothes and I soon realized I did not have much to contribute. I felt a bit ridiculous when we were out together and no one noticed me at all.

The first day I could hardly wait to take them on a tour. Le blonde La Donn wore a leather mini, red tights, and high heels, and didn't understand why I thought she should see old buildings and dirty markets. She kept tripping off her shoes into potholes on the sidewalk, and complained about things she felt were not up to her standards. We never went touring together again.

Azuri was a beautiful brunette, with sparkling brown eyes and light skin, long fake fingernails and thick hairpieces. Few people manage to look natural in such things, but Azuri decorated herself with such expertise that she seemed born to beauty. La Donn and I marveled at the array of beautifully beaded costumes that Azuri brought to Colombia; she willingly let us borrow them whenever we asked. Azuri got along with everybody, even Mr. Zeytun.

Neither La Donn nor Azuri liked to join me on jam-packed busses or visit questionable neighborhoods, and they didn't care for the inexpensive eateries favored by the locals. Once again, I ended up hanging around with Colombians.

The cashier at the Libano, Germán ("Hermán"), was sweet and good looking but ridiculed by his coworkers because he was gay. We shared a passion for soft cuddly things like puppies and teddy bears.

"You are honest about your lifestyle," I said one day. "Is it difficult here, to be gay?"

"It is lonely."

"But you are one of the kindest people I know. You must have many friends."

"People criticize. Sometimes they attack me on the street."

"I haven't met many gay men here. Where are the others?"

"There are many, but they lead two lives. You won't find many who admit it. Just look around—would you?"

In a country known for swaggering Mafiosos and heavily armed soldiers, I could see that it took great courage for Germán to be openly gay.

Through my friendship with German I met many supposedly straight men, men who had wives and children but engaged in other tendencies secretly.

"Why don't you just tell the truth about your preferences, like Germán?" I asked one of the closeted gay men.

"I could never tell my friends or families," he said. "Homosexuality goes against the church."

"Why marry? Why not just live discreetly, as a bachelor?"

"Marriage was expected of me," he said, and added, quite matter-of-factly, "I did it to show my family that I am respectable. Otherwise, they would think I am immoral."

"But what about the woman? Divorce is not acceptable here. Is that fair to your wife?"

"We do what is expected of us," he said.

And, I thought, *you lock a woman into an insincere marriage with no exit mechanism.*

More than ever, I appreciated Germán's courage.

I also met Lucho, an ex-hippie photographer who had just finished a film about Colombian street kids. Lucho was a rebel—though he came from a wealthy Colombian family, he was eager to hang out with all kinds of people in diverse locations and he absolutely rejected class restrictions. Uninvolved in politics, but very intellectual, his opinions tended to lean left.

"Where can I go to see some interesting things?" I asked.

"How about Egypt?" he said.

I soon realized that Lucho was the perfect person to ask— Egypt was one of Bogotá's worst neighborhoods. We took a bus to a crumbling collection of run-down pastel colored buildings clinging to a hillside, with streets full of rural people; women in hats and long braids, men wearing *ruanas* (blanket-like garments similar to *ponchos*).

Seeing the little *gamines* begging us to buy trinkets, I told Lucho about Oscar.

"So many children live—and die—on Colombia's streets that we made a film about it, hoping it might help us find solutions," he said. He spoke quietly, pausing for emphasis. "We estimate that there are over *40 million* street children in

South America. Sometimes they band together in groups with other homeless kids, sleeping in boxes and under bridges and behind park benches."

"Those gangs used to steal Oscar's toys," I said.

"Sure. They don't always behave perfectly. These kids are desperate to soothe hunger and rejection. They beg. Sometimes they steal."

While we were picking our way through dogs and chickens, I studied Lucho. He was totally unlike any affluent Colombians I had met before. Wealthy Colombians simply did not "dress down"; even when they wore jeans, they opted for designer styles that looked distinctly expensive. If there were any conservative old crones in Lucho's fancy family, surely they choked on their crumpets when they saw him striding along in his handicrafted clothes, boots, T-shirts and old jeans.

"Are you planning to work on more films?" I asked.

"I plan to go to New York City, where I will become a filmmaker," he said. "See there? That old church has Rubens paintings on its walls."

I hurried after Lucho, struggling to keep up with his long, lanky stride, to enter a disintegrating church with beautiful artwork.

"You really don't mind visiting places that haven't been sanitized for tourists, do you?" he asked.

"I love it! Where else can I go?"

"Why not Villa de Leiva?" he suggested. "I think you'll

find it quaint, old fashioned. Start by hopping on a bus to Tunja."

We headed back towards the *residencia*. Now that I had a destination in mind, I could hardly wait to finish my dance assignment.

When I got back to the neighborhood of the restaurant, I decided to try one more time to find Oscar. I tracked down the hot dog vendor and asked him if he knew where Oscar had gone. "An American lady came to take him home," he said—the most crushing answer he could have given, because I knew he was just trying to make me feel better. There was no American lady, and if there was any good news about Oscar, he would have told me. Oscar was gone.

I became closer friends with the head maid, Nina. She couldn't read or write, but she hungrily devoured TV news and asked a never-ending stream of questions of foreigners staying at the *residencia*, carrying on worldly and astute conversations while making homemade sausages. Luckily, I was not yet a vegetarian, so I enjoyed her *morcillas*—sausages made of cooked blood. I loved Nina's cooking! One of my favorites was her home-cooked version of the Bogotáno specialty, *ajiaco*, a soupy stew made of chicken and vegetables. After it is served you put avocado slices, sour cream and capers on top and eat it with little *arepas*.

I often went to the maid's quarters in the *residencia*,

where Nina and I talked about anything and everything.

"Have you ever been married?" I asked.

"Ah! Better off without him," she said, dismissing the subject. But whatever had happened obviously did nothing to dampen Nina's zest for life.

"I'm going to make a party for everyone. Will you join us?" asked Nina.

"Of course!" I replied.

She brought out a record player and put on music.

"Come on," she said briskly, "Everybody dance!"

Putting awkward Americans at ease almost instantly, Nina stepped forward in her cushiony white maid's shoes to take foreigners by the hand, teaching them to dance the *paso doble* (a Spanish dance—rather old fashioned for Colombians at the time). Eyes twinkling, she supervised a roomful of foreign adoptive parents, belly dancers, and maids and then served a marvelous dinner.

11

*"I plan to walk down
the street and catch a bus
out of town," I said.
This shocked everyone
in the restaurant.*

In Colombia, they called anybody who was involved with
semi-organized illegal activities a Mafioso, whether they were
a thief or a drug lord. Drug trafficking was implied, but never
directly talked about. However, the Mafiosos from Barranquilla
did seem to have a particularly ferocious reputation.

We didn't see drug use at the Libano or around any of our
regular haunts. Traditionally, except for an ancient coca-leaf
chewing tradition among indigenous peoples, Colombia had
never been involved in drug activity—until the 1960s, that is,
when the USA's demand for marijuana skyrocketed. At first,
the USA fed its exploding appetite for marijuana through
Mexican connections, but when the DEA* tried to eradicate
US-Mexican trafficking, it accidentally crowned a new drug
kingdom: Guajira Peninsula, on the northern tip of Colombia.

Barranquilla is a port city on the north coast of Colombia.
During my stay in Bogotá, vast quantities of drugs (supplied
by the Guajira Peninsula) were being shipped out of
Barranquilla to the USA; Barranquilla produced fearsome
Mafiosos, and Guajira spawned their steely-eyed bodyguards.

Mr. Zeytun was scared to death of these guys. When they
came in, he rolled out the red carpet and perspired until they
left the restaurant. I don't know if they were likely to do any

* **The Drug Enforcement Agency, the USA's primary anti-drug
organization**

of us physical harm, but I couldn't help overhearing talk about their nefarious activities. There was no doubt that the Barranquilla Mafiosos were high echelon drug smugglers, and they were among the characters that made me glad our contract was nearing an end.

As our month drew to a close, I mentioned my plans to Mr. Zeytun.

"The day after our last performance, I'm going exploring," I said.

I knew that his mellow business facade hid a compulsive need to control, but he seemed to accept my idea. Before leaving the restaurant, though, I saw him take an employee named Luis into his office, a habit of Mr. Zeytun's that always foreshadowed complications. Mr. Zeytun liked to handle problems indirectly through Luis—a yuppie yes-man who seemed to have absolutely no character of his own. All Luis ever did was parrot back whatever we said, adding whatever Mr. Zeytun wanted him to say.

Not long after he emerged from Mr. Zeytun's office, Luis approached me.

"It is a better idea for you to stay and do another contract," he said in his thin, reedy voice. Tall, pale-skinned, weak-looking Luis wore little round wire glasses and came from Antioquia, a very white place where people are called *paisas* and have old-fashioned Spanish accents.

"Luis, I've been planning to travel for a very long time."

"Yes, traveling would be very interesting," he agreed. Mr. Zeytun signalled to him, and after a short discussion with our boss, he sidled up to me again.

"Traveling in Colombia is too dangerous. You and Azuri should stay and dance for one more month," Luis ordered meekly. "But La Donn complains too much," he added. "We should bid her good-bye."

If Mr. Zeytun told Luis my shoes were made of goat cheese, he'd never question it, he'd just repeat it on cue. I had no respect for him at all, and I told him so.

"Luis, the closest thing you have to an opinion is whoever is nearest to you," I said.

That confused him. Apparently Mr. Zeytun didn't tell him what to think about that, so he just stood there.

"You make me sick," I added.

From then on, Luis avoided me and Mr. Zeytun had to talk to me directly. He tried to force Azuri and me to stay and do another contract, but I was tired of his controlling ways.

"No, I don't want to stay for another dance engagement," I said. "I plan to walk down the street and catch a bus out of town." This shocked everyone in the restaurant.

When we weren't performing, Mr. Zeytun ran a leisurely operation. As friends came in and sat around, talking, he would have waiters bring Arabic coffee (called "Turkish coffee" in Miami). On this particular day his wife was relaxing with us. She was a delightful woman, though quite spoiled, and seemed far more attached to her manicures and perfect clothes than to her own opinions. I could not tell if she was more shocked by my refusal to cooperate with her husband's wishes or the unthinkable idea of sitting on a bus with regular people.

"Impossible!" said Mr. Zeytun. Luis wasn't there to buffer his objections, and this talk of bus-riding was getting out of hand. His relaxed manner disappeared. "Either you stay and work for me," he said, "or you leave Colombia, period!"

"No way!" I protested.

"You will stay, or I will speak with friends, who will deal with you as a troublemaker." His friends, I assumed, were the people who he had paid off to handle customs issues and visas.

"It would be best if we stayed," said Azuri.

12

When I walked in, there <u>he</u> sat—muscular, rugged, wearing jeans and cowboy boots.

We stayed only long enough to fulfill our original agreement. Before we could make a break for it, a down-to-earth, genuinely nice Syrian man named Nedim showed up at the restaurant after driving seven hours from Neiva, a small city in southern Colombia, by jeep. Nedim hoped to hire us for an Arabic festival he was organizing.

"These are *my* dancers," Mr. Zeytun said, implying that he, personally, owned us and could take full credit for our skills, looks and brains. "I am their agent," he added. As I look back, I can understand his possessiveness. After all, he paid for our tickets to Colombia. It would have been reasonable for him to ask for a commission, though he seemed more intent on giving Nedim the runaround.

Poor Nedim sat around the Libano for two days waiting for our boss to make a deal with him, but Mr. Zeytun ignored him completely and stayed in his office, sending employees out now and then to offer vague messages of encouragement.

"What are you doing?" I asked Mr. Zeytun after watching Nedim sip what must have been his hundredth lemonade.

"I'm too busy to bother with the man," he replied.

Apparently Nedim really wanted dancers at his festival, because after sitting around the Libano for two days, he made a 14-hour round trip and returned to Bogotá with his lawyer, a dashing young man named Esteban.

When I walked in, there *he* sat—muscular, rugged, wearing jeans and cowboy boots. I caught my breath and immediately pulled up a chair, trying to look businesslike. But before I could ask a single question, he spoke. In a wonderful take-charge voice, Esteban addressed Mr. Zeytun:

"Are you going to let them do Nedim's festival or not? Stop playing games."

Mr. Zeytun was used to being in charge, but could not dominate this casually bespectacled cowboy lawyer. Looking resentful and beginning to sweat, Mr. Zeytun looked at his gold watch, unconvincingly feigning a busy schedule.

Esteban stood his ground. "Do the deal now—or drop it!"

"My dancers ... work only for me," Mr. Zeytun finally replied, sounding uncertain.

"Then just say so! Don't mess with my friend." And then Esteban, the hunk, turned his full attention to *me*. Nedim introduced us.

Esteban's wide-open grin perfectly complemented his powerful personality.

"May I come see you this weekend?" he asked.

"I won't be in town long. But why not?" I replied.

We went to his favorite restaurant, an all-night place where they served food from the Bucaramanga area, a locale renowned for its unusual gourmet cuisine. Esteban courted me steadily while I finished my dance contract with Mr. Zeytun.

Not surprisingly, Esteban had become a *persona non grata* at the Libano. Mr. Zeytun suddenly refused to speak to me. In view of the allure of not one, but two adventurous travel ideas—Villa de Leiva (Lucho) and Neiva (Esteban)—I was more than ready to pack my travelin' bags.

La Donn left, or so we thought. Unexpectedly, she showed up again at the *residencia*, dreadfully upset, nearly hysterical. "They won't let me go home!" she whimpered. "It's Mr. Zeytun's fault! At–at–at the airport. They said–they said I can't leave Colombia!"

As we tried to calm her, we pulled a story out of her that further eroded my already jaded impressions of Mr. Zeytun. Employers, we learned, were required to pay an exit tax on their foreign performers. Unless Mr. Zeytun paid his taxes on us, none of us could leave.

We thought that if the taxes weren't too high, we might be able to get them paid somehow, but even that was not possible—along with taxes, the employer was required to fill out documents, and only Mr. Zeytun could complete the documents or sign the forms. He had not handled any of this for La Donn, and didn't bother to tell her either. She arrived at the airport with a plane ticket that officials would not let her use.

Since I was the one that spoke Spanish, I had a talk with Mr. Zeytun. "You haven't paid your taxes," I said. Mr. Zeytun crossed his legs, taking care not to crease his carefully tailored

Dallal

suit. His hands, adorned with several expensive rings, were folded on one knee.

"My taxes are not your affair," said Mr. Zeytun.

"Well, if you have a problem with La Donn's complaining, maybe I should bring her here to express her opinion."

He didn't seem to mind, shrugging his shoulders. He paid La Donn's taxes, but Azuri and I quickly discovered that the issue wasn't resolved. Trying to get us to agree to another dance assignment, Mr. Zeytun continued to threaten our departures, knowing that Azuri wanted to visit historic Cartagena and that I wanted to hop on a bus for places unknown.

"No. I will not hear of it," Mr. Zeytun decided on our behalf.

"We're going sight-seeing and there is nothing you can do about it," I retorted.

"Then I won't pay your taxes. You'll never get out of Colombia."

"I'm going anyway."

"We'll see about that!"

"I'm going to visit Esteban in Neiva."

It took a lot to make the dapper Mr. Zeytun turn red in the face, but apparently I pushed his buttons with that statement. Looking like I'd spat on his kingly shoe, Mr. Zeytun began to yell, his voice booming and clapping through the restaurant like an echoing blunderbuss. I whirled to walk away from him and went straight to the *residencia* to pick up my suitcase.

Not long afterward, Mr. Zeytun showed up at the *residencia*, flanked by a group of three guys in dark suits, looking all puffed out like they were on some mission of critical importance.

"Either you're going to work for me or you're going to get out of the country!" he said.

"Then pay my taxes and let me out of the country!"

I had a real smart mouth back then, although before I left South America I did learn to tone it down. At that time I thought I could just say whatever I felt, but the time would come, much later, when I would get myself into situations where back-talk was just too dangerous. Mr. Zeytun, for his part, was so used to controlling women that he had no question he was going to win this battle. He could not imagine that any female would flatly refuse to cooperate when he exerted his will.

"*Que pasa?*" asked Nina, standing next to me protectively. Seeing Mr. Zeytun standing there with three bullies, she did not back down one bit. Watching Nina, you'd think she confronted blustering men about the exit taxes of belly dancers two or three times a day; she was absolutely serene, though I could see from the tight little line her lips formed that she found Mr. Zeytun's antics unacceptable.

"Mr. Zeytun won't pay my exit taxes."

"I see." When Mr. Zeytun got tired of talking and left, Nina took me inside and telephoned one of her many contacts, this time, a man who was a top lawyer at the DAS (an agency in Colombia comparable to the FBI in the United States). She cupped her hand over the phone. "He owes my family a favor. Let's see what he can do."

Thanks to Nina, the matter was resolved—Mr. Zeytun was taken at gunpoint to visit with DAS officials and paid his taxes on the spot.

NEFARIOUS ACTIVITY LOCATOR

Guajira Peninsula

COLOMBIA

Barranquilla

Cartagena

Pamplona

Medellín

Bucaramanga

Zipaquirá

Tunja

Ibague

Bogotá

Cali

Villavicencio

Popayán

Neiva

Tumaco

Pasto

E C U A D O R

Ipiales

Tulcan

Guerrilla
Activity

Drug
Distribution

13

*I stepped backward
three centuries — the
only movement was a
man and his burro.
The only sound
was an echo*

My heart pitter-pattered for Esteban, but trekking around
South America was my goal so I had no intention of halting
my travels in Neiva, where he lived. It just wasn't my time to
stop traveling. But he was waiting for me and I promised to
visit.

Mr. Zeytun made one last effort to dominate. "I have
friends all over Colombia and I know where you're going," he
warned. "They will find you and take you off the bus. You'll
be arrested."

"I'll be down south, in Neiva. Esteban will look after me,"
I replied. And then I hopped on a *buseta* heading north
towards Tunja for a loosely planned rendezvous with Lucho
in Villa de Leiva.

*Busetas** are miniature public busses that maneuver well
in the mountains and can squeeze by other vehicles on narrow
winding roads. The bouncy little *buseta*, filled with women
whose long braids emerged from little black hats to fall
straight onto hand-loomed woolen skirts, and cheerful men in
rope sandals and *ruanas*, soon entered the *departamento*
(state) of Boyacá. It was exciting—just what I had wanted
from the moment I first set foot in Colombia. We jiggled
along through old colonial towns, nuzzling velvety green hills

* **Don't use the word buseta in Brazil. There, it refers to a private
anatomical location.**

Dallal

filled with emerald mines.

Changing *busetas* outside the cold mountainous town of Tunja seemed like mayhem. Bus drivers competed for passengers by yelling and beseeching us to choose their vehicles — each of which inspired less confidence than the next.

A lady going to Villa de Leiva seemed to know what she was doing, so I stuck with her for a short but treacherous ride. We sped up and down switchbacks, dodging oncoming trucks and skittering along the edges of drop-dead cliffs, gasping at the breathtaking views.

My bus wore a glittering multicolored sign that said, "*En las manos de Dios*" ("In the hands of God"). Another bus advertised, "*Jesus Cristo nos protecta*" ("Jesus protects us"). Like the Colombians, I came to have faith in my destiny.

Behind the bus driver were clusters of hanging black bags. People took the bags, barfed and casually tossed them out the window. Pom-poms danced over the windows and lively music blared. Black bags lined the mountain roads.

The land gradually shriveled up into parched stone roads and desert scrub. Then Villa de Leiva sprouted, an oasis—the fertile green crops encircling the town were dotted with wandering animals; exquisite fragrances from parks abloom with colorful flowers wafted through the open windows in our *buseta*. Every white house blazed with crimson barrel-tile roofs.

The solid stone plaza, which seemed immense for such a

small town, equaled the size of a football field, amplifying every sound in its emptiness. The first time I set foot on the plaza I stepped backward three centuries; the only movement was an old man and his burro, the only sound was the echo of their footsteps.

I liked that plaza a lot, so I checked into the old hotel that faced it. For US $2 a night it wasn't a bad buy, despite my tiny room with two undersized beds and a non-closing window facing a wall. Down the hall, the bathroom offered a cold water shower and another permanently open window. I was glad that my room had two beds, because when I turned down the covers of the first, the sheets were covered with bug larvae.

"Lucho!"

The next evening, in a flower-filled park, I ran into my friend.

"I thought you'd be coming here," he said quietly. We took off for a magical midnight motorcycle ride through olive groves. When we stopped to savor the moonlight, I asked Lucho more questions that no one else seemed to want to answer for me. "Lucho, how did Colombia's class system get so entrenched?"

He seemed relieved. "I'm glad you question Colombia's class system. Most Americans are content to transition right into the upper class scene, where everyone is trying to imitate Americans anyway. Tourists come here from the USA, a country that claims it endorses equality, but the minute they get here it all goes out the window."

"Yeah. I've seen ordinary Americans come here and suddenly feel high class. But sometimes I get idealistic notions. I've made a few mistakes."

"Like what?"

"I wanted Nina, the maid from the *residencia*, to come to the restaurant. I looked forward to performing for her, thinking it would be a treat for her. But even though I offered to pay for it, she just never showed up. One night she finally did come, but she was uncomfortable and felt like she didn't belong—she didn't dress like the others. People gave her haughty looks as she sat there, alone. Everyone knew she was from a different class. No one was comfortable. I didn't do anyone a favor."

"I could have predicted that. You see, it's not that simple. Our class system has a long history; it's like a set of doors that are nailed shut. That's why attempts to open the doors have been so violent," he said.

"So how did it get that bad?"

"Colonial society placed *People From Spain* (known as *peninsulares*) at the top of the heap, giving them exclusive access to political power. *Descendants of People From Spain*, called *criollos*, were allowed to hold less important political positions. *Mestizos*—people of mixed Spanish and Indian heritage, were not allowed to hold political positions at all. Below the *mestizos* were Indians, and least valued of all were black slaves from Africa. Our class system evolved from these colonial power hierarchies."

"Even after hundreds of years, people still are stuck with all these class restrictions," I said.

"Yeah. And it has spawned four centuries of political violence."

Lucho was a thinker and a dreamer, and as we zigzagged through the whispering trees I found myself wondering how these qualities would show up in his films.

"Are you really going to New York?"

He assured me that he was.

"Let me know how to contact you. I'd like to visit you when you get to New York."

We returned to the echoing plaza, and soon Lucho rumbled away.

Colombia's Class System

5%	Upper class
20%	Middle class
50%	Lower class
25%	Sub-lower class

Colombia's tiny upper class still holds political and economic power. If you own lots of land, have a distinguished family lineage, or made a fortune as an entrepreneur you might get invited to the upper class.

What's a sub-lower class? Also called "the masses," these are the illiterate and impoverished, who cling to the margins of subsistence.

An interesting conflict arises for women as they reach higher economic status. The higher the status a woman achieves, the more restrictions are placed upon her. Upper class women are stuck with rigid marriage expectations. Women of lower classes aren't saddled with chaperones, and they often have more freedom to dump dysfunctional men.

14   *"Don't worry about the guerrillas. I know them."*

Esteban lived in a small town outside Neiva, in an area marked "not recommended" by tourist agencies. But very few places seemed to be "recommended," so I searched for transportation south to Neiva and discovered a *buseta* filled with crowds of singing, *aguardiente*-drinking people headed to the "Bambuco Festival." What excellent timing this was— my trip to Neiva coincided with one of Colombia's major folkloric festivals! The San Pedro ("Bambuco") Festival is held annually and features parades, beauty pageants, concerts and folk dance competitions. No one could have been more delighted than me—I *love* folk dancing and music, and as the passengers in our little *buseta* sang along with an assortment of regional songs, I knew I was in for a treat. Our traveling party lasted until 2 a.m.

Rain poured down as we arrived in Neiva, stirring the dusty streets into brown soup. The driver dumped our suit-cases in the mud and bolted away like a drenched cat.

"Can you drive me to El Rancho Verde?" I asked a taxi driver, searching for transportation to the little hotel managed by Esteban's family, tucked away into a tiny town outside of Neiva.

"All right. If you pay me double."

"Why should I have to pay double?"

"It's late, the roads are empty and there are guerrillas."

"Oh."

"Do you want me to take you there or not?"

"Sí."

"Then you pay double."

There was nothing to do but accept, so I hopped into the car and handed him the amount he demanded. Several people, including those at the American Embassy, had warned me about guerrillas in the Neiva area, but when I asked Esteban about it, he seemed unconcerned. "Don't worry," he had said, "I know them."

It never occurred to me that the dashing Esteban might behave differently at home, or that traveling into remote areas might prove awkward if you decided to leave the guy.

Soon after I arrived, I realized that most of Esteban's brothers were terrorists; one was in prison and another was a Soviet-trained organizer for a guerrilla group called FARC.

"I thought you were a lawyer." I said.

"Yeah, I am ... well, not really a lawyer, but I went to law school for awhile." He explained that he practiced a sort of unofficial law. As he talked, I gathered that his not-quite-sanctioned legal services were used mainly to get his brothers out of trouble.

"What is 'FARC?'" I asked.

"FARC. *Fuerzas Armadas Revolucionarias de Colombia.*"

"Revolutionary Armed Forces of Colombia. You are revolutionaries?"

"I'm not political, but my brothers are Marxist-Leninists, and yes, revolutionaries!"

"How big is your operation?"

"Well, it's not my operation. FARC came about when '*Tirofijo*' ('Sure Shot') Marulanda Vélez got together with Communist Party members in 1966. The Communist Party gave money and weapons, and FARC recruited people. They

Colombia's guerrilla organizations (1980s)

FARC — Fuerzas Armadas Revolucionarias de Colombia (Revolutionary Armed Forces of Colombia). The largest Colombian guerrilla organization.

M-19 — Movimiento 19 de Abril (19th of April Movement). The most internationally connected guerrilla group in Colombia, and prone to the most outrageous acts.

ELN — Ejército de Liberación Nacional (National Liberation Army). Considered to be the most effective of Colombia's guerrilla groups.

EPL — Ejército Popular de Liberación (Popular Liberation Army). The only Colombian guerrilla group spouting Maoist ideology.

Quintín Lamé Command — A small guerrilla group; supported by Colombia's Indian populations.

organized six thousand peasants and now it's the biggest revolutionary group in Colombia, didn't you know that?"

"Do they attack anybody?"

He grinned.

"Sí."

"Who? Did anyone die?"

"They sometimes attack military posts. But my brothers just organize and recruit."

"What are they trying to accomplish? Do you think FARC can defeat the Colombian Army?"

"They stage their attacks to collect ammunition. And they get a *lot* more weapons." Esteban tipped his wooden chair back precariously, lacing his fingers behind his head, well-muscled legs confidently straddled. "They've grabbed tele-communications equipment too!"

"Oh. Who finances them? The Russians?"

"Nah. The Soviets don't help much with money. But they trained my brother Carlos, and many of the organizers. FARC has its own ways of getting money. Rich people should share with the cause."

"What do you mean?"

He didn't answer directly, but I gathered that FARC handled cash flow problems by kidnapping wealthy people for ransom.

You'd think that Esteban's connection with FARC would protect him from guerrilla kidnapping threats, but it did not.

As the youngest child of a prominent family, Esteban was on the blackmail list of another guerrilla group called M-19.

"Wouldn't you get farther if you worked together?" I asked.

"They aren't Communists. They were Rojas Pinilla people."

"Who?"

"Rojas Pinilla was Colombia's only dictator in a couple hundred years. He was kicked out, but his political party kept running in elections. M-19 is more socialist than Communist."

"What does 'M-19' stand for?"

"Aah. They named themselves after April 19, 1970, when they claim an election was stolen from their party. They responded by organizing a revolutionary group."

"What's different about them and FARC?"

"For one thing, they formed alliances with Cuba and Nicaragua. Cuba admits it; they helped M-19 with recruiting, especially in the cities. M-19 has us out-organized in urban areas."

"If your brothers weren't in FARC, would they be in M-19?"

"No, see, FARC is a lot bigger than they are. Besides, you wouldn't approve of M-19—they're violent."

"Why do they want to kidnap you?"

He paused. "Well, Tami, guerrilla groups are funded like this: 'You, as a wealthy person, pay us a monthly fee. In return, we won't kidnap any of your family members.'"

"Are you wealthy?"

"Not really, but my family owns a quite a bit of land, and we have prestige. Since I'm the youngest, I'm the family favorite. That's why they designated me as the kidnap target. We pay them a fee every month."

"Preventive ransom."

"I guess so."

Politicians or businessmen might have a problem living in the midst of Colombian guerrillas, but I didn't feel frightened. Although there were periodic violent attacks, most guerrilla activity concentrated on disseminating information and converting local people to their cause. Guerrilla groups were looked upon by many as political parties, and in some small towns, guerrillas held their meetings openly, right in the middle of the plaza.

FARC changes its activities almost as often as performers switch costumes. The last chapter of this book tells of FARC's evolution into a mainstream political party—but FARC is now involved

New Report from Dallal... in new violence.

Use the order form on page 169 to get Dallal's FREE new report. Includes TRAVEL TIPS for Colombia, where to buy cumbia music, the latest on FARC ... and more.

The Bullets of M-19

- 1974: M-19 stole Simón Bolívar's sword and spurs from an exhibit.*

- 1976: M-19 kidnapped and murdered a Colombian trade union official accused of ties to the CIA.

- 1979: M-19 tunneled into a military weapons cache in Bogotá and made off with 5,000 guns.

- 1980: M-19 seized and occupied the Dominican Republic's Bogotá embassy, and held it for 61 days.

- 1981: Cuba admitted its involvement in an M-19 terrorist operation in southern Colombia.

- 1985: M-19 attacked and wounded the Commanding General of the Colombian Army

- 1985: M-19 carried out its infamous siege of the Palace of Justice, Colombia's Supreme Court building. More than 100 people were killed, including 11 judges. The building was destroyed in heavy artillery fire.

- 1986: M-19 tried to create a multinational guerrilla front with Peru's "Shining Path," the "Tupac Amaru Revolutionary Movement," also of Peru, and Ecuador's "Alfaro Lives, Damn It!"

- 1988: M-19 kidnapped a two-time presidential candidate.

- 1989: M-19 decided to establish itself as a mainstream political party, the "Democratic Alliance M-19" (AD/M-19).

- We will never know if Timothy McVeigh's lawyer discovered this coincidence, since he was not allowed to use a defense pinning the Oklahoma City bombing on international terrorists. M-19 stands for: April 19. The date of the deadly Oklahoma City bombing: April 19, 1995.

* Simón Bolívar is credited for liberating most of South America from European colonial control.

Dallal

*Esteban and his friends — the
Colombian equivalent
of rednecks — continued
their drunken binge,*   **15**
*yelling and getting violent,
ignoring the women.*

Ironically, Esteban's Communist-oriented family—while engaging in guerrilla revolutionary tactics to abolish class privileges—treated their many servants like dogs. Whenever anyone in the family clapped or whistled, the nearest servant came running. Some servants were as young as ten years old. I asked, and was told they were of a lower class, and therefore did not go to school. I suppose Esteban's brother Carlos, the Soviet-trained FARC organizer who was most involved in the cause, couldn't see his own hypocrisy when he treated the servants with even more disdain than did other family members.

Communism might have its merits, in theory, but I don't like what I've seen of it in practice. When I went to Cuba I met lying and privileged government officials and miserably bored workers who lived in poverty—both sides kept looking for ways around the system. I can hardly imagine such a disorganized place as Colombia coalescing into Communism, but I can understand its appeal. Communism may be the only way many poor Colombians can visualize unlocking their rigid class system.

I prevailed on Esteban to take me to the festival, which turned out to be a disorderly parade of cars carrying beauty queens from each of Colombia's *departamentos*. People drank huge amounts of *aguardiente*, peddled on the street in enormous quantities. They didn't even pause to pour it into a cup—just guzzled straight from the bottle. Rowdy drunks blundered around and motorbikes putted among the pedestrians, their riders frequently falling off or tipping over.

Esteban joined the ranks of stumbling inebriates, swigging enthusiastically from his bottle of booze. I hadn't acquired a taste for *aguardiente* and soon was the only sober person for miles, and perhaps also the only one with any comprehension of traffic safety. Along came a friend with a motorbike.

"Let me borrow that," said Esteban. "Come on, Tami, let's go for a ride!"

He could barely stand upright and I wasn't ready to chance losing my legs. "No." Drunk men turn me off. I couldn't wait to leave.

The next day, Esteban and his group of friends—who, I had come to realize, were the Colombian equivalent of rednecks—took me to the local "exclusive" country club: restaurant, swimming pool, nice, dull. The men continued their *aguardiente* binge, yelling and swearing and getting violent with each other while ignoring the women.

When we got back to the ranch, I decided to take the next bus out of town. That's when I discovered there was no transportation back to Neiva, and realized that no one in Esteban's family would take me.

Esteban's mother had a talk with him, and he promised to stop getting drunk and neglecting me. The next day, hoping that Esteban's immensely improved behavior would hold out for a few hours, we attended a five-hour open air folk dance competition.

Each group of 20 or more musicians and dancers represented a different region of Colombia. A *cumbia* group from the Pacific Coast really inspired me, with haunting music and a dramatic dance depicting two men dueling for a woman. All the dancers had deep mahogany skin—the women in bright red-and-white checkered skirts, the men in knee-length pants, sandals, crimson checkered shirts and big straw hats.

The dancers' hips fluttered like beating wings to *cumbia's* compelling sounds, born when African slaves met fluid Latin music. While *cumbia's* melodic construction feels Hispanic, components of its harmony are reminiscent of Colombia's Indian cultures; its fascinating, compulsive backbeat, however, comes directly from Africa. Said to come from the era when slaves were chained at the ankles, forcing them to drag their feet as they walked, distinctive shuffling dance steps traditionally accompany *cumbia's* pulse.

The men enacted a dramatic fight, spinning around hitting machetes against each other. A huge black coffin with a cross on it appeared, flanked by women who shuffled so smoothly that they appeared to float. They synchronized movements with lighted candles as they glided, ghostlike, across the stage. Feeling like I was part of a drama in a faraway jungle, I watched them enact the loser's funeral with an entirely convincing theatrical flair, and dreamed that one day I might stage a Mid-Eastern dance performance as powerful as this magnificent Afro-Colombian dance.

The next day, we attended a *correleja*. They closed off an entire street, set up bleachers by the road and released bulls one at a time. Amateur drunk wannabe bullfighters taunted and harassed the bulls as the crowd shouted insults and threw garbage. Young mens' bodies were so loose from days of drinking that they easily recovered from falls, but I saw several potentially fatal near-misses when enraged bulls charged. Esteban thought he should go fight a bull. Once again I threatened to leave—this "sport" was so mindless, cruel and unskilled that I finally lost patience with it. "They're just having fun!" Esteban protested as I walked away.

"I hate seeing human dignity, and the bull's dignity, reach such a low level," I said.

After that there was no chance that Esteban, who it turns out was really a hog farmer, not a lawyer, would take me to his hog ranch. He personally supervised the slaughterhouse and had decided I was too sensitive to see what happened to what I considered to be his cute piggies.

We visited "El Jardin," our Syrian friend Nedim's restaurant, a sparkling-white hacienda on a well manicured piece of land which had once been a ranch. People dined outside on rustic wooden furniture surrounded by bright flowers. As I sat there, eating pseudo-Arabic food, created with a sincere attempt at authenticity but lacking the proper ingredients, I looked up to see vivid colorful canaries singing in cages.

Nedim was a wonderful host, with his rustic, friendly manners, genuinely appreciative that we had come. Later, I agreed to dance for his patrons, though I soon regretted my offer to dance, because rain began to pour down and the only place to perform was outdoors. But Nedim had wanted so badly for people in his town to see Mid-Eastern dancing, and was so proud that he had found a belly dancer, that I decided to dance anyway, in the drenching rain. My dripping performance was, to say the least, unconventional.

Nedim showered me with appreciation. After two 14-hour round trips and several days of disrespect at the Libano, I was glad that this kind man at least had something to show for it.

Nedim's sweet disposition did much to keep negative stereotypes at bay, since I met several obnoxious Arab men while in Colombia. In America, and in the Arab countries I later visited, Arabic people are usually considerate and kind.

Something about Colombia's wild frontiers attracted foreigners interested in quick money. While there was no doubt that many foreigners in Colombia were less than scrupulous, I did find myself wondering if, a hundred years ago, the United States "Wild West" attracted equally unsavory characters. Probably.

At Esteban's ranch, we ate a traditional holiday ranch dinner—barbecued pig followed by orange and grapefruit peels soaked in sugar syrup, served with cheese. Delicious!

I didn't mind leaving Neiva. Although Esteban was now on his best behavior, he no longer charmed me the way he had while courting me in Bogotá.

*Thawing in the dewy gold
of dawn, I watched
the sun rise over
rolling hills and
coffee plantations.*

16

Wary of Mr. Zeytun's so-called "friends," I took off on a zig-zag pattern through Colombia. Having discovered that Esteban lived in the midst of a guerrilla stronghold, I felt certain Mr. Zeytun wouldn't dare to bother me there, but I made sure my travel plans were unpredictable now that I was leaving.

I took a short trip south to San Augustin, where people ride horses through hills to view gigantic stones that ancient Indians carved into faces. For a fee, a child offered to show me the sights. I rented two horses, requesting a calm horse—calm, yes, but mine was ridiculous. An exhausted old mare who kept falling asleep on the job, she stumbled on loose stones and, but for my vigilance, would have sleepwalked right off the abrupt edge of a steep hill.

Delighted when the tour was over, I took the little boy up on his offer to visit his home. They lived in a poor shack with newspapers tacked to the walls to keep people from seeing through wide cracks between boards. His mother was very sweet and had many children. She baked breads to sell in the open market. Her husband? Unemployed. Drank all day.

By then, drunk men were really starting to irk me. Having lapsed into a mood of some disenchantment with men, I caught myself thinking: *Yeah, this is par for the course, this guy.* I assigned the blame for the family's poverty to him because he was drinking all day and not contributing.

Cartagena

Azuri had raved about Cartagena, insisting that I must not miss out on it. I headed toward the northern coast, a trek of 40 hours and five *busetas* across most of Colombia.

The first *buseta* was driven by a man who spent more time fixing the tape deck than looking at the road. It was very crowded so when I wasn't standing I held a chicken on my lap.

On the second *buseta* I sat next to a musician returning from the festival and we had a lively conversation.

"Why is Cartagena so popular?" I asked.

"Because it oozes history," he said. "A Spanish explorer named Pedro de Heredia arrived in Cartagena in 1533; Cartagena was a refuge from Indian attacks and the Spanish used it as a base for exploratory expeditions, so it has a big fort and a lot of historic colonial buildings. Tourists love to see those old structures, as well as the beaches."

"I guess, since it's on the ocean, it became a shipping center," I said.

"Yes. But Mother Spain would not allow her colonies to trade with each other. Even if they were right next door, colonies first had to send the items to Spain; then Spain would reship to the neighboring colony."

"Well, if I was one of Mother Spain's children, restrictions like that might cause me to run away from home."

He laughed. "Then you and Colombia have a lot in common. Spain's selfish trade restrictions helped to motivate the liberation of Colombia."

The third *buseta* was an all night roller-coaster, barreling back and forth on switchbacks through the mountains and traveling at such high altitude that I froze all night. While thawing in the dewy gold of dawn, I watched the sun rise over rolling hills and coffee plantations.

The political significance of queasy roads ...

Colombia's politically disenfranchised masses—estimated at 50 to 75 percent of the population—have not been able to form a cohesive political base, except through guerrilla tactics, because a barely-there highway system makes it almost impossible to connect with each other. Only recently have highways been carved into Colombia's mountainous terrain.

Three parallel mountain systems break western Colombian highways into a serpentine mess; potholes caused by cold weather make one question whether Colombia's three main highways can really be called "paved." Although many roads are being added, vast areas remain inaccessible.

The trucks and busses we dodged now were merrily painted with bright pictures. Many carried overflowing loads of bananas, trundling along like some exotic new species of tropical-hued beetle of particularly gigantic proportions. My stomach heaved, but I didn't want to miss any of the scenery. I didn't have the guts (Ha) to ask for a barf bag, although the girl next to me tossed her cookies several times, flicking little bags out the window as casually as cigarette butts.

Two more bus changes and another night on the road brought me to Cartagena. At 5 a.m., after 40 hours on the road, I felt dizzy and grouchy and somewhat less fresh than an Irish spring. My enthusiasm for travel adventures had waned, and all I wanted to see was a bed. Hotels were booked up, in the clutches of peak summer tourist season, so a nice taxi driver went door-knocking on my behalf and I ended up sleeping in a preschool.

The next day I set out exploring. Cartagena is a city in two sections: the mainland, where poor neighborhoods surround the historic colonial seaport near a downtown area filled with colonial Spanish buildings; and the peninsula, a wealthy resort area sparkling with new hotels, restaurants and soft sand beaches. I was feeling quite anonymous until ...
Urk!
I turned on my heels, looking for an excuse to avoid a man standing near a little sun-baked garden. I had seen him in Bogotá, where he kept interrupting me as I tried to savor a

rare piece of chocolate cake. In Colombia I could find very little good chocolate, and excellent fudge cake was out of the question until I found an exclusive café that featured divine baked goods. I used to go there just to eat cake. One day an American man wandered into the café and started snapping pictures of me, never asking permission, until finally I asked him what he was doing. He said he thought I was pretty, and that he wanted photos of pretty Colombian girls to take home with him.

Why did he have to show up in Cartagena? Hastily, I planned my escape ... too late! Now he had seen me.

I knew it would be difficult to get rid of him, but I noticed United States Air Force men swarming all over Cartagena, so I attached myself to a group of military types, striking up a casual conversation.

"What are you guys doing here?" I asked a handsome six-foot Puerto Rican-Italian officer from Alaska.

He grinned and came closer, coming into step with me. "Vacationing. We're stationed in Panama."

Perfect. We began to walk together, dissuading the clingy American camera-bug from approaching. My new Air Force friend took me out to dinner, and later we clip-clopped through the moonlight in a horse-drawn buggy, meandering around Cartagena's historic streets under twinkling tropical stars.

17 *"I'm sorry, your ticket is no good," said the Eastern Airlines representative.*

I meandered back in the direction of Bogotá, planning to spend the rest of my money on leisurely explorations before flying home.

There was Pamplona, the city of students. I went to a restaurant reputed to be Pamplona's very best, a simple place, the only eatery in town that offered salads. Apparently they thought I was odd, because the waitress had to ask the owner if she could serve me. They weren't used to women dining alone. They turned out to be quite friendly, however—everyone in the kitchen came out to watch me eat.

And there was Giron, a postcard-perfect colonial town, where a woman invited me to *once* ("ohn-say"), the traditional Colombian afternoon tea, where one partakes of hot chocolate and tamales. Gypsies camped by the old drawbridge, the women wearing long skirts and, if they were married, scarves in their hair.

There was Cucuta, where I was turned away from hotels for being female. "It is the policy," they said. "Single women are not allowed." It happened three times in a row. My duffel bag was getting heavy, and their males-only mindset made me feel dejected and offended.

And there was Bucaramanga, which I dubbed the city of unusual food.

I arrived in Bogotá thinking I'd pick up my other suitcase at the *residencia* and fly home. "I'm sorry, your ticket is no good," said the Eastern Airlines representative. "You can only go as far as Panama City."

"What about Miami?" I asked.

"Your American travel agent made an error on the Panama-Miami portion."

"What kind of error?"

"An error from which we cannot recover the ticket."

I called Mr. Zeytun and asked him to fix the mistake, but he seemed to think it was very funny. "Hah! After sending goons after me with machine guns, you want *me* to help? Forget it!"

I had run out of money.

A Bucaramanga Menu

1. Rice cooked with goat's blood. (I tried it, but it wasn't my favorite.)
2. Milk soup with fried eggs in it. (Quite good.)
3. Arepas (The best in Colombia; large and golden-colored with a touch of salt.)
4. Fried ants (I missed that; apparently this dish is a springtime specialty.)

18

*Someone hacked
the gold mine's
manager to pieces.*

A new Arabic restaurant called "El Khalifa" had opened
nearby—even fancier than the Libano, it had a doorman-
bouncer-security guard who dressed like an Arab, with white
flowing robes and a black-and-white checkered head piece.
He attracted much attention from people driving by as he
showed customers where to park.

I walked up to the owner of El Khalifa, a sourfaced man
named Hassan who didn't like anyone or anything. He was a
thin man with salt-and-pepper hair and he spat when he
talked. Keeping my distance, I suggested that he hire belly
dancers. Nabil, an assistant, stepped in.

"I like your smile," he said, and hired me without ever
seeing me dance.

Had Ali Baba himself whisked me off on a magic carpet, I
could not have landed in a more enchanting little restaurant.
El Khalifa was straight out of an Arabian dream, its windows
capped in Moorish arches, pointed at the top; fancy Arabian
carpets cushioned my footsteps as I danced by the bronze
artwork and intricate lamps that were scattered throughout. A
little rock garden decorated the center of the restaurant. When
people dined in the banquet rooms on the second floor, I
danced up the spiral staircase to entertain them, then back

down to the main floor.

We arranged to hire a band and dancers from the USA, but the Colombian government interrupted our plans by declaring "National Artist's Month." Surprise! Everyone with an Artistic Visa was told they must stop working for the next month. Someone had complained that foreigners took away jobs, and so it was decreed: employment of foreign artists must halt for 30 days. I argued that there were no Mid-Eastern dancers in Colombia so I wasn't nudging anyone out of a job, but no one cared. Fortunately, in three weeks of dancing I had saved $500.

I could have gone home, but we had already arranged for a new troupe of performers and Hassan, despite his grouchy attitudes, wanted me to continue dancing for El Khalifa. Besides, something itched. Images of Colombia's back roads and *busetas* had begun to tempt me once again, and a 30-day forced vacation could accommodate a lot of bus tickets!

I am a member of a group called "Servas," an international friendship program where travelers stay in members' homes for three-day stretches. My Servas roster listed an elderly couple in Ibague, a city south of Bogotá that looked much like America in the 1950s—big rounded cars, clunky radios and old fashioned stores. It was in Ibague that I first tasted *avena*. *Avena* means oatmeal, but in this beverage the oatmeal was very finely ground and bore no resemblance to anything I had ever tasted before. They suspended the particles in hot milk and flavored them with cinnamon—wonderful!

Doña Olga lived in a small apartment with her maid. Her husband, Don Alberto, was often away tending to his gold mine. You had to ride horseback to access the gold mine, tucked into a hillside outside of town. While I was visiting, the manager of their mine got hacked to pieces by machete-wielding thieves—either thieves, they said, or possibly he had been caught with somebody else's wife—anyway, the old couple had their hands full. I traveled on to Calí.

On the night I rode between Ibague and Calí, I had a whole seat to myself, and thought, *Good, I can sleep!* But my seat was a smooth vinyl bench and we passed through a very mountainous area called Armenia—every time the bus took a sharp turn I slid back and forth, nearly landing on the floor several times. Sleep proved impossible. I ended up spending the entire night clutching the seat in front of me.

Boisterous bus rides featured other challenges. I was afraid of missing my little black barf bag so, when feeling queasy, I taught myself to close my eyes and fall asleep instantly. I also discovered a great anti-nausea medicine: Colombian Coca Cola. In every country, Coca Cola seems to have a different taste—in Colombia, it was thick, syrupy-sweet and spicy, and it cured queasiness.

A
COLOMBIAN
Road Map

Barranquilla

Cartagena

Pamplona

Bucaramanga

Medellín

Villa de Leiva

Tunja

Ibague

Bogotá

Villavicencio

Calí

Neiva

Popayán

Tumaco

Pasto

Ipiales

Tulcán

ECUADOR

bouncy hairy (gasp)

MOTION SICKNESS INDEX

*It must have been in Calí
that this bond had
formed, etching itself
into my soul before
I was born.*

19

Calí

The moment we rolled into Calí that curious sense of familiarity returned. This time it electrified me. A sense that I had
lived here before tingled through every pore; the closer we
got to downtown Calí, the stronger the sensation became. By
the time the bus stopped, I knew the streets and what to
expect coming around each corner, a feeling so powerful that
I simply dropped my luggage at the nearest hotel and set out
walking.

I recognized every street and park in the downtown area.
How could this happen? Only a few newly-built shops and
storefronts were unfamiliar—somehow, the city of Calí had
etched itself into my soul when I was a child, or even before I
was born. But how?

Returning to the hotel late that night, however, I realized
that my intuitive knowledge of Calí apparently wasn't enough
to help me avoid this place. It reminded me of a horse stable,
with rustic double doors on my room that I had to chain
together and padlock. Soon after I lay down to read, I realized
that I might want a weapon, and eyed my sword. First were
the sounds of couples having vociferous sex—dozens of

them, moans and screams, echoing off walls and reverberating through halls. Then there was a fight. Then somebody was shaking my flimsy padlocked doors.

"Do you want Coca Cola?" he asked beerily.

I ignored him.

"Let me in! I have Coca Cola!"

"Go away!"

"Let me give you your Coca Cola. Open the door!"

My sword got into bed with me and I tried to sleep. The next morning I looked up Luz Maria, another Servas contact, a Colombian woman who was married to an emerald dealer. Her brother, a gorgeous cowboy, invited me to the family ranch, and wrote the following instructions on how to get there:

"Take the bus from Ipiales toward Tumaco ... Get off 20 hours later at a fork in the road ... hitch a ride to Candelijas on a cement truck ... ask the owner of the general store to hail a passing canoe ... then take the canoe to the ranch."

I promised to visit and they said they would be waiting.

20 *People had warned me to watch out for the "Indios bravos," the fierce Indians.*

Guambia

Tall slender men wearing bright blue skirts and hand-loomed black-and-pink ponchos filled every seat on the *combi** as it carried us to Silvia, their town. I had seen them often in Bogotá selling their handicrafts on the street, with their clear cinnamon-colored skin and fine features. I thought they were a beautiful people.

Most of the Guambianos conversed in their own language, but a man sitting nearby shifted to Spanish so we could share stories.

"The Spanish began to take away Guambiano land soon after they invaded our homeland. Then they sold our land to colonists, who built haciendas. By their law, we were "contracted" to work for their newly established haciendas a certain number of days each year. The Spaniards set up *resguardos* (reservations), forcing us to move farther and farther into the mountains, freeing more land for their haciendas."

"We have something like that where I come from. Indian reservations."

"Yes. But Guambianos do not accept it. We fought back,

* A combi is a public transport van. It keeps no set schedule—combis just wait in a designated spot to gather passengers. When full, they head out.

organizing groups of up to 4,000 Indians to take back the haciendas that had displaced our people. When the army challenged us, we outwitted them and fought until they gave up. Finally, the Colombian government compensated the hacienda owners for their losses, and we reclaimed our ancestral land."

"Has it been difficult to pass your language and customs along to your children?"

"At first, officials would not allow our children to wear Guambiano clothes to school, so we converted some of the haciendas into our own schools. Now our children attend school wearing Guambiano clothes, and we teach them the Guambiano language as well as Spanish."

Well intentioned people had warned me to watch out for the *Indios bravos*, the fierce Indians. So far, they seemed soft-spoken and friendly, though assertive.

We arrived on market day. Colorfully painted busses filled with Guambianos poured from nearby mountains, everyone dressed exactly alike save the quantity of beads around the women's necks. Like the men, women wore little bowler hats on their heads and construction boots on their feet, and the same brilliant blue wool skirts. Women draped strings of thick glass beads around their necks to indicate economic position—the more beads, the wealthier they were. Often, they shopped by bartering rather than exchanging money.

Always busy, Guambiano women spun wool even when walking and talking. Each carried a bag of fleece over her shoulder and a held stick in her hand wherever she went, rolling the fleece into yarn and wrapping the yarn onto the stick as she walked to and fro, or as she sat selling handi-crafts. I rarely found groups of people in Colombia that I could describe as "well organized," but the Guambianos were.

I checked into a small family-run hotel, feeling poorly and looking haggard.

"Are you all right?" asked Pedro, the owner, when he noticed that I had barely any voice, red eyes and a runny nose.

"I just have a cold."

Pedro suggested a visit to the medicine man and offered to take me. His wife wasn't thrilled at the two of us setting off together on his motorcycle, but I assured her she had nothing to worry about and soon Pedro and I rumbled away to Guambia, a rural area deep in the hills where only the Indians live.

Though I don't know his private life, the small middle-aged medicine man was more female than male in his person-ality and mannerisms. He enjoyed traditional female roles of child rearing and nurturing; he cooked and sewed and spun wool into yarn while walking. His womanly ways did not seem to bother or intimidate anyone. In fact, he ran a kinder-garten and cared for an adorable two year old adopted son—apparently, the Guambianos didn't worry about feminine tendencies being contagious.

Dallal

We went into a windowless room full of eucalyptus branches with a pungent bonfire in the middle, where the medicine man prepared *agua de panela* with mint. *Panela* is made from squeezing the juice out of sugarcane, then cooking it for hours until it becomes a hard brown lump. Cutting small pieces off his dark, sweet lump of *panela*, the medicine man melted them slowly in hot water, adding just the right amount of fragrant mint. I wanted to ask many questions, but he seemed to prefer his own language, and my throat hurt. Gently, he handed me a serving of the warming drink, beckoning me to sip it as I sat by the smoking eucalyptus. We sat together silently in the overwhelming smoke, drinking *agua de panela* and sweating. My cold improved tremendously.

When we hopped on the motorcycle to return home, Pedro discovered the headlight had burned out. We knew we wouldn't get far on a blinded motorcycle, but Pedro and I agreed that it was in the best interests of his marriage to get back to Silvia that night, so we set out walking.

When you are in an area with no electric lights and only a sliver of moon, the nights are so dark that you can see nothing at all. You cannot see one foot in front of the other, so you stumble along blindly, hearing footsteps approaching, unable to see whose they are. It seemed to take hours to become accustomed to the dim starlight. When my eyes finally adjusted to capture the tiny bit of available light, I saw people all around, returning from market day. Many of the men were drunk and staggering.

As we trudged into town, aching and footsore, we saw men sleeping off their alcohol consumption on benches, in the grass, on sidewalks.

"The introduction of *aguardiente* was no favor to the Guambianos," Pedro muttered.

Everyone (except Pedro's wife) had gone to bed by the time we arrived.

Perhaps the medicine man will not exist after a few more decades. In my Colombian experiences, only a few people seemed to believe that indigenous peoples have the right to protect their traditional way of life, and what limited government "protections" there are for Colombia's Indians, now comprising only one percent of Colombia's population, seem designed only to assimilate them. I felt a profound respect for the Guambianos as they struggled to preserve their customs in the face of almost overwhelming odds.

Colombia's Ethnic Groups

Mestizo (mixed white and Indian)	58%
White	20%
Mulatto	14%
Black	4%
Mixed black-Indian	3%
Indian	1%

Dallal

When we got to the middle
of the lake, my boat's rude
pilot beached the boat   **21**
on an uninhabited island.

Popayán

From Silvia, I traveled to Popayán, a once-beautiful and
historic city, destroyed the year before by an earthquake that
shook apart 1983's Easter celebration.* Popayán, I was told,
used to have cobblestone streets and white colonial buildings.
The earthquake must have been terrible, because Popayán had
been renowned since colonial days for its *celebración de la*
Semana Santa (Easter week celebration). People traveled to
Popayán from all over Colombia to attend Mass and participate in costumed processions.

Studying the rubble, I tried to imagine what this ghostlike
town had looked like before the earthquake. The crumbled
stones seemed, somehow, intimate, and this puzzled me, until
I realized that the quake-jumbled city reminded me of something beyond old colonial buildings. Popayán's ruins demonstrated our ancient connection with Earth herself.

Hoping Mother Earth was comfortably readjusted, I
looked for a place to stay, booking a room for just one night at
an empty partially renovated hotel. At nightfall, without
electricity, this once-bustling city was almost as dark as

---

* **Popayán has since been restored, and today is considered a
picturesque destination for those seeking off-the-beaten track
places to visit.**

midnight in Guambia.

On my way to the bus station the next morning, at least 100 troops of soldiers dressed in camouflage piled out of army trucks and posted themselves on every street corner. They scoured the broken city carrying machine guns, looking for ... who knows what? I hurried to the bus station and never did find out.

Pasto

On the road to Pasto a patchwork of crop colors on odd-shaped plots clung to the mountains like a clumsily-tiled mosaic. I wondered why, in this idyllic setting, the *Pastuchos* (people from Pasto) had been selected as the butt of Colombia's ethnic jokes. I suppose every culture finds someone to ridicule, for whatever reason, though in Pasto I couldn't help but feel that *I* was the odd one.

I never gave it much thought, but I kind of got myself into trouble there. No hotel would rent to a woman traveling alone, but I managed to persuade an old fashioned rooming house to give me a room. It was a men's-only place, so I found myself trying to ignore men's backsides as I brushed my teeth while they peed in urinals.

The next day, after hearing about a beautiful lake, I set out to find a ride to it.

"I am looking for passengers," said a man with a taxi.

"How much do you charge?" I asked.

He opened his pants and started masturbating. Next!

I joined a vanload of people, and we bumped along until the driver dropped us off in a small town, where I hopped a milk truck to "The Port," a collection of small lakefront wooden houses which served fresh-cooked trout while local boat owners hustled for customers.

"Where do those boats go?" I asked.

Nobody could give me an explanation, but they all suggested that I go—so I went. When we got to the middle of the lake, my boat's rude pilot beached the boat on an uninhabited island.

"We must renegotiate the fee," he said.

"We already agreed on it."

"You are mistaken. That is the fee to take you only to this spot."

I looked around—no one in their right mind would commission a boat to this nowhere place.

He glared stubbornly. "Pay me now."

"I already paid you!"

"Pay me now or I will leave you here."

It was pay or be stranded, so I paid.

"And money for gas."

I handed him an extortionate number of *pesos* and we traveled on to dock in an enchanting spot with a building in the distance.

"Where are we?"

"Go to your hotel."

"That building?" I pointed to a distant structure perched on a hilltop.

He ignored me and shoved off. Dragging my heavy duffel bag, stuffed with beaded costumes, a sword, tape deck, a sewing project, makeup, toiletries and clothing, I struggled through a marsh and up a tediously long hill to end up at a honeymooner's retreat.

The Swiss owner guessed (correctly) that my boatman had no intention of retrieving me the next day. In this romantic hideaway, filled with couples who wanted complete privacy, there was nothing to do but eat meals at prescribed times and sit by the fireplace at night. I felt stifled and out of place.

I had so little to do that I found myself listening to other people's conversations.

"Look, that's her!" a woman's voice exclaimed.

Who were they talking about? I looked over and saw a family pointing at me.

"Aren't you the dancer from the Libano?"

"Yes."

"What are you doing here?"

I didn't care to admit that I had hopped into a boat without knowing the destination, nor did I relish an explanation of why I selected a solo excursion to a honeymoon hotel.

"Sight-seeing," I offered.

Dallal

"How long will you stay?"

"Actually, I'm ready to go back now. Do you know how I can get back to Pasto?"

"Certainly! You must come with us."

After thanking my new friends and waving them off, I looked around Pasto's shabby bus area full of unfortunate misshapen people, some crippled, some unusually short, some looking malnourished and ... well ... inbred. I caught a rickety unupholstered bus to Ipiales, a town on the southernmost tip of Colombia on the Ecuadorian border, the first stop in my directions to the ranch.

A nibble of Ecuador

People told me I couldn't get into Ecuador without giving up my hard-earned Artistic Visa, but I wanted to see how far I would get. Besides, Luz Maria's family had told me about yummy Italian chocolates made in Ecuador, and finding them had become one of my priorities.

Colombians and Ecuadorians crossed the border without passports and nobody checked *their* papers. My hair was dark, and I bought my sweaters and boots in Colombian stores just like everybody else. Young Colombian women wore the same hair style as I did, and their olive-toned skin wasn't so different from my own. Most people thought I was Colombian (until I talked), so I headed for the bridge between Colombia and Ecuador and kept my mouth shut, hoping no one would question my oversize duffel bag, planning a look of wide-eyed innocence if they caught me. I put on a nonchalant expression and merged with the crowds to cross the border bridge, then hurried onto an Ecuadorian bus to the nearest town, Tulcán.

The landscape kept growing prettier—green terraced hillsides dappled with the slanting rays of morning sunshine managed to outshine similar scenic places in Colombia. The bus stereo played contagious *cumbia* music, just slightly different and even more enticing than Colombian *cumbia*. I immediately liked Ecuador.

Tulcán was a typical border town—one street lined with shops selling things you couldn't find in Colombia: cheap silver jewelry, woven clothing, blankets, bags, and chocolate. I bought silver jewelry and hand-woven textiles for my friends and family and then set out in search of Perugina *baci* chocolates.

Colombian chocolate was waxy and flavorless. Here in Ecuador, a gourmet chocolate factory had been built by the famous Italian company, started by an entrepreneur from Perugia Italy who had invented a chocolate version of heaven in 1907. He spun *bacis* out of finely chopped hazelnuts and whipped milk chocolate, topping each confection with a hazelnut—but he was not finished. He coifed these little treasures in rich bittersweet chocolate and dressed them for the opera in classy silver and blue foil fashioned by Italian designers. *Bacis*—"kisses," in Italian—whisper romance and often come packaged with love letters.

Enough about *bacis*; I found the Perugina store and bought some *bacis*, only to discover even more sinful choices. Perugina roasts its cocoa beans using some sort of secret formula to produce a unique aroma and taste. Then they grind their perfectly toasted beans and slowly conch the chocolate to create an ethereal melting texture. Yum! I purchased several generously sized bars of bittersweet Perugina, hiding them deep in my duffel bag hoping they would lie there forgotten, the better to reach my friends in Bogotá.

Waddling out of the chocolate factory, I tried to buy a bus ticket on to Otavalo, a town from which many of the Ecuadorian Indians I had met at Bogotá markets came.

"Passport, please."

I feigned innocence. "Oops!—I was supposed to have my passport with me?"

"You can't continue into Ecuador without your paperwork."

"Sorry—I'll go back." Sheepishly, I turned north to return to Colombia.

On my way back to Ipiales I stopped at *Santuario de Nuestra Señora de las Lajas*, a majestic, remote and reputedly miraculous sanctuary nestled into cool mountains with a river running underneath. Well, saying the river runs beneath doesn't really do its adventurous architects the honor they deserve: the church spans a stunning gorge, the Guáitara River rushing along through dizzying depths below the sanctuary.

The Virgin Mary, legend has it, appeared there in person in the 1800s. It is said that she was seen on a tremendous rock perched high above the river. That rock, and the statue of the Virgin that still remains, crown the sanctuary as its highest altar. Not surprisingly, this imposing mountain church begets miracles. I saw locks of hair and gifts left to thank the saints for *Santuario de las Lajas*' most recent miracles.

The gothic church, with its two tiers of tall arched windows, a steeple as tall again as the building, and dozens of smaller spires covering its tapered roof, seemed uniquely Colombian—a contemplation, in a nation of contradictions.

I woke up on a bus full of snoring men, stuck in the middle of the jungle.

22

The road to the ranch

It was time for a schlep through the jungle. In Ipiales I caught a bus headed for a bumpy dirt road through the dark jungle that led to Tumaco. It seemed easy enough. Then, in the middle of the night, we ran into a driving rainstorm and the windshield wipers didn't work. Apparently trusting in his abilities to maneuver an unseeing vehicle through trees and curved embankments, and bent on keeping his schedule, the driver barreled along as if only weenies used windshield wipers.

As dawn glimmered through the jungle, we stopped at a thatch-roofed wooden hut, passengers piling off to buy warm soda and breakfast: plain rice and fried eggs. I could see from the contents of the store that jungle provisions were slim so I dug into my duffel bag and snacked on a Perugina chocolate bar instead.

When we got a flat tire I noticed there was no spare, so I wondered what they would do. In case you're wondering too, here's how it goes: all the male passengers get out, and that means everybody but me, and they all stand by the side of the road smoking cigarettes and offering advice. Then the driver uses a patch kit. Everybody piles back into the bus and off you go—until the next mechanical problem.

Every few miles, the bus broke down. Cigarette smoking men helped the driver pour gasoline from a big can into the carburetor and the bus stumbled a little further.

"Don't worry, we'll coax her to Tumaco," the driver said.

"Will the owners fix the bus in Tumaco?" I asked.

"No, no. I won't tell the owners. The company charges me for repairs so I turn in my bus without reporting problems."

They were very messy with the gasoline, which they carried inside the bus. Once, while taking a cupful of gas for the carburetor, they spilled it all over the floor. No matter. Passengers lit fresh cigarettes.

People stepped in the gasoline, spreading it everywhere. Soon most of the men on the bus were smoking. Terrified at the prospect of blowing up and unable to contain myself any longer, I blurted a warning: "Gasoline fumes can explode when you light a match."

They laughed.

"Tell them not to smoke near the gasoline! Please."

The driver scoffed.

"I'm going to hitchhike," I said, gathering my bags to get off the bus.

"Hah! Hitchhike! A woman? We cannot allow it," the whiskered men exclaimed.

"I'm getting off!"

Dallal

"That is not safe," they insisted, flicking ashes on the fuming floor.

I prayed while everyone else relaxed, gossiping and enjoying the fresh air between mechanical failures. Finally, trusting that we were all *en las manos de Dios*, I went to sleep. When I woke up I realized that I was alone in the midst of a bus full of sprawling, snoring men, stuck in the middle of the jungle. Even the driver was asleep. Then I saw that we were caught in a traffic jam, with cabs and busses clotting the road as far as the eye could see ... ahead of us, a truck had exploded. Something about a gasoline fire.

Even after the explosion, the men continued to slop gasoline around—smoking, chattering, chuckling. Half-panicked, I reviewed my instructions:

– bus through jungle

– fork in road

– cement truck

– ask man at general store

– canoe to ranch

I reminded the driver of my destination anxiously (and often); he said the same thing every time: "Yes, there is still a ways to go." If searching for a fork in the road by peering out a window can make it show up any faster, I'm sure I hurried it along several minutes.

We stopped at a tiny side road, and I got off—no road signs, no identification whatsoever; I could only hope it was the right place. My instructions were to wait for a cement truck, so I sat on my duffel bag and hoped to recognize one if I saw it.

A rumbling and squeaking contraption pulled up next to me.

"Excuse me, sir ... are you a cement truck?"

"Sí. Going to town?"

"The town with the general store?"

"That is the only town," he said.

Candelijas was a chocolate-scented jungle town, with squat wooden shacks lining the one dusty street, and burlap bags filled with cacao beans laid out to dry in the sunshine. The whole town smelled like raw sun-warmed cocoa.

The general store looked like it belonged on a stage set in a vintage Western movie: staple goods, canned food, and weapons were scattered helter skelter on the shelves and a wealthy old man with a huge belly stood behind the counter.

"They said you can find a canoe to take me to the ranch," I said, trying to give the impression that I was browsing.

He mumbled something gruffly. But then he poured hot coffee into a tin cup and sprinkled it with powdered milk. "Certainly. Please, make yourself comfortable," he replied, handing me the cup with a kindly smile.

I looked around and saw that his store sold just about anything you could want in this remote area—generators, mosquito nets, guns, fishing equipment, even hot coffee.

Dallal

Taking my steaming cup outside to sniff the chocolate air, I waited. By and by, a canoe approached.

"Are you going to the ranch?" I asked.

"Sí. Get in."

It was a chore for me to lug my loaded duffel bag, now bursting with presents, to the handmade wooden canoe, but the muscular canoe pilot lifted it one-handed and hove it into the boat.

Soon we were paddling down a murky tributary into the jungle, gliding as silently as a crocodile though the dull mud-brown water; a sunless sky, dark and overcast, winked now and then through our tunnel of green and brown foliage. We were surrounded by an almost oppressive silence, tattooed here and there with brief, rhythmic paddle splashes and occasional flutelike bird calls. Dense vegetation offered its own special perfume, newly sprouting, slowly decaying. My T-shirt stuck to my back and everything everywhere seemed to drip.

23

They walked between the palm trees singing African music with Spanish lyrics.

Several ranch hands and a German Shepherd met us at the river's edge and escorted me to a simple house.

Jorge, Luz Maria's hormone-inducing cowboy brother, came riding in like a vision from a romance novel. He was rugged, gorgeous and had a good education, just my type. Unfortunately, he was married, though he complained that his wife rarely joined him on the ranch. I felt a great temptation to smile alluringly at this neglected man, but never gave him a hint the whole time I stayed in his candle-lit house, so sadly lacking a woman's touch. The unattainable Jorge behaved like a perfect gentleman.

Walking was too squishy, so we went horseback riding on narrow dirt roads, mostly under several inches of water. I wondered if our horses missed the crisp *clip-clop* their hooves would have made on firmer surfaces—here, each step sounded like a plumber's friend unclogging a drain. *Shhloop ... squoosh ... slurp!* Caramel colored cows munched vegetation in swampy fields.

Most people in the vicinity of the ranch were of West African descent.

"Did Colombia have slaves?" I asked.

Jorge filled me in on Afro-Colombian politics as we

Dallal

slopped along.

"Yes. At first the Spanish used *mitayos* for laborers–"

"–*mitayos*?"

"Indians contracted to work for the crown."

"They enslaved the Indians?"

"No. Technically, they were free, because they got paid. But it was only a token salary, not enough to give them any economic strength. And the owners of mines and haciendas literally worked them to death. Colonists decided that, since the Indians couldn't survive their working conditions, they needed another source of cheap labor. The crown granted some people 'licenses' to become slave traders."

"I didn't realize that South America was involved in slavery."

"Yes. The Spanish brought Africans into the port of Cartagena and sold them to miners and hacienda owners."

"How long did slavery last?"

"Well, by the 1600s, all of the Indians working the mines had been replaced by black slaves. Then plantations, like yours in USA, became important, so the demand for slaves kept increasing. Slavery wasn't abolished until Colombia won its independence from Spain in the early 1800s."

"I haven't heard anybody talk about racial tension in Colombia."

"It's a little different here than in the USA. Our geography offers many inaccessible places, so a lot of slaves were able to escape. Both the mountains and the jungles protected large populations of runaways."

Jorge interrupted to point out acres and acres of palm trees, lined up like rows of swaying soldiers. Each bore clumps of orange-colored nuts.

"Our ranch produces palm oil," he said. "We press the palm nuts to extract a thick orange oil used for cooking."

His father had built rather fascinating oil-pressing machinery, entirely out of old train parts. After processing, they poured the palm oil into huge metal tanks, which they loaded onto barges that came twice weekly for transport to Tumaco.

Except for Jorge and a few workers brought from Calí, almost everyone I saw was black. They walked between the palm trees singing Nigerian music with Spanish lyrics in richly booming voices that carried great distances.

"The music here seems to be based on Conga drum," I said, "unchanged from the music of West Africa, except that they sing in Spanish."

"Yes. Their ancestors escaped soon after arriving here, preserving their music," Jorge responded. "Did you know that runaway African slaves were the first people in South America to declare independence from Spain? You should see the Choco province—it's an area north of here, along the Pacific Coast of Colombia. The Afro-Colombian population there is so culturally separated that anthropologists come from all over the world to learn about them."

Dallal

Since there was no public education on the ranch, the bookkeeper, a handsome young man named Vicente, created a makeshift schoolhouse out of a tiny ranch building. People came from all around—small children, adults, anybody who wanted to learn. When I attended class one day, I noticed that a teacher's assistant kept getting the alphabet letters mixed up. Nowhere did I see a single sign, newspaper or book, so I suppose reading was a novelty. A little learning was probably better than none, but illiteracy, unfortunately, can translate into exploitation.

I noticed oil drills pumping away nearby. When I asked about it, my hosts named a powerful international super-corporation and told me that, no, it didn't hire local people; yes, the friendly local people shared what they had, charging nothing for the use of their land; no, they didn't seem to mind. Unable to read, people in this remote jungle area could not capitalize on employment advantages. With no reason to obtain newspapers, they didn't know that other people prosper when they own land that produces oil.

People who live simple lives in rural areas are often perceived to be happy and carefree. In this modern world, however, fueled by corporate power and money, people risk their traditional lifestyles if they don't have a chance to get wise.

We ate something terrible for supper, like rice and spam. All ranch food came out of a can except the fresh milk, warm, beige and creamy. I brought out my Ecuadorian chocolates and we feasted the evening away watching old fashioned soaps on a generator-powered television, the jungle version, I suppose, of an evening at the opera. By the time I left the ranch, every last morsel of Perugina chocolate had vanished.

Exports

Colombia brings in about US $6 billion each year in exports. Depending on who you talk to, one of these three products leads all the others:
- **Coffee**
- **Illicit drugs**
- **Oil**

Other powerful products include:
- **Cut flowers**
- **Bananas**
- **Cocoa beans**
- **Oilseed and palm oil**
- **Emeralds**

Guerrillas revolutionize the oil industry

Unbeknownst to me, a guerrilla group shared my concerns about foreign oil exploitation. The ELN guerrilla organization began to target the oil industry in the mid-1980s, forcing the government to pay attention to foreign corporations' exploitative oil policies. ELN wanted Colombia to terminate multinational explorations—and they were effective.

They started with kidnapping foreign oilmen, then escalated to bombing oil pipelines and attacking refineries. The ELN carried out over 100 attacks within a single year, disrupting the entire national economy, so Colombia tried to use its military to defend pipeline operations. Disorganized truckloads of khaki-uniformed boys, however, were no match for ELN's guerrilla tactics. In the late 1980s, a Colombian organization called Ecopetrol took control of all of Colombia's oil pipelines. Ecopetrol still owns most of Colombia's oil wells, but foreign oil firms now participate in some joint ventures.

Other ELN activities: The ELN also seized control of small towns, opened jails to free prisoners, and robbed banks. Everyone was impressed when ELN persuaded Camilo Torres, a prominent Roman Catholic priest, to join their cause— but he was killed by the army. Any mutual affection between the ELN and the Roman Catholic Church evaporated in 1989, when the ELN assassinated the Catholic bishop of Arauca.

24   *Garbage flowed right in*
the open door of a house.
This happened twice a day,
every time the tide rose.

Gloria, the ranch manager's wife, wanted to go to Tumaco to
deliver a bag of beans. I wanted to go there because the
thought of another 20 hours in a jungle-beaten bus appalled
me and Tumaco was the only place that offered a flight back
to Bogotá. While we floated downriver in a canoe to Candelijas,
Gloria applied a full face of makeup. (See? I'm not the only
one who wears makeup in the middle of nowhere.)

Since Gloria's bag of beans was even bigger than my
duffel bag, we struggled mightily until a man the color of rich
Colombian coffee effortlessly tossed both bags over his
shoulders and loaded them into a jeep. We had to stand up all
the way to Tumaco, jolting along in the back of the overflowing jeep clutching a bar, inhaling the road as clouds of dust
billowed up, ruining our makeup.

Tumaco

Tumaco was an unwashed armpit. A shockingly poor town, it
sat on an island which had been de-elevated several feet by an
earthquake. High tides flooded the community twice a day.

Some thatched-roof houses were built on stilts, while
others should have been. I watched as garbage flowed right

Dallal

into the open door of one house when the tide rose. Even when tides receded, currents were such that they did not carry the sewage away; instead, it simply eddied around to return (and multiply), at the next high tide.

As people cooked their dinners by the fetid water, children with open sores waded and played in the muck. The men I saw in Tumaco looked healthy and strong—their bodies must have developed incredible defense mechanisms to survive, I surmised, though I wondered how many children never reached adulthood. Or, perhaps, after generations of germs, the Tumaccan people had evolved some sort of super-powered immune system?

One neighborhood was accessible only by boardwalks. The whole town was grubby, but I thought it would be interesting to wander around so I went exploring. The farther I walked on the maze of planks, the more boards had rotted away; soon three out of every four were missing, so that every time I looked down I saw waves of stink sloshing gently below. It made me a bit sick. Then, as I stood on this alien structure, a hidden splendor revealed itself on the horizon: a dull sunset shone through the colorless sky, stubbornly beautiful, like a warm smile on a warted old woman.

Seeing my tenuous attempts to straddle the creaking boards, some women sent their children over to help me. So sweet and willing, they held my hands and guided me confidently from one shaky piece of wood to the next, skipping along easily and telling me not to worry.

I feared that a bargain-priced hotel in this festering hole of a town might not be fun, so I opted for Tumaco's finest hotel, a fancy US $7 a night (as compared to my usual $3 or $4); this bought a tiny room with a terrible sewage stench.

Vicente, the ranch bookkeeper, motorcycled over to take me dancing at Tumaco's hottest club. We rode to a tinsel-decorated two-room cinder block disco that served Coca Cola, beer and *aguardiente*. Sitting on folding chairs on a bare cement floor, we listened to a record player blasting sultry Afro-Latin rhythms and Michael Jackson songs.

Crippled in one leg from polio, Vicente had a complex, imagining that nobody liked him because of his withered leg. He was angry so much of the time that people who knew him stayed away. Though he could dance quite well despite his partially disabled leg, he self-consciously urged other people to dance with me; then he moped because I danced with them. I felt compassion for Vicente, but when he got drunk and very sour, I simply ignored him.

As the evening died, I sat quietly, soaking up my last moments of exotic tropical funk, knowing I would fly back to Bogotá in the morning. I was not about to let somebody else's complex get me down.

Perhaps I saw Tumaco without her makeup—tourist guides describe a place that sounds quite different:

Tumaco for tourists

"Famous for its beaches, with three enchanting islands, where many tourists play," says one guidebook. "A paradise of tropical music and dance," gushes another. "Wonderful food—fresh fish and abundant crustaceans," says one more.

Tumaco is said to be famed for its beautiful women—one, Stella Márquez Zawasdski, was crowned "Miss Colombia."

Athletes and soccer players from Tumaco have triumphed all over the world. Silvio Salazar, winner of the famous international race of San Silvestre; Marino Klinger, Luis Eduardo "Tumaco" Gonzalez, and Wilinton Ortiz, the best Colombian "agile" of all time, lead the list.

Office politics unveiled: price haggling Hassan, gossiping musicians, a sabotaging secretary, a thieving bus boy and booby-trapped juice.

25

El Khalifa

When the enforced idleness of National Artists' Month ended, I joined my new troupe of performers to resume work back at El Khalifa. Hassan was cheap and wanted the best artists for half what they were willing to work for, but he didn't like to put himself on the spot.

"Talk them down, they are asking too much."

"But they are asking the usual rate," I explained.

"Pah! It is robbery, what they ask. Tell them!"

And so it went, with acid-personality Hassan on one side and high strung musicians on the other. I could never seem to negotiate pay low enough to suit Hassan or high enough to satisfy the performers.

Hassan found his own *oud* player, a man named Mohammed who seemed to particularly detest me. Mohammed liked to spend all his discretionary time entertaining a circle of Arab men who loved gossip and believed whatever they heard. And at El Khalifa, office politics began to worm its way into the sequins and bright lights.

After listening to Mohammed, a secretary who had been friendly to me began to sabotage. Knowing that I danced to taped music at lunch, since the musicians only worked at night, she erased parts of my tapes, leaving surprise blank moments to hang like naked holes in my choreography. When I made new tapes and punched out the corners so they couldn't be erased, she found a button on the stereo which would speed up and slow down the music as it played. At first I couldn't figure out why my good tapes sounded like chipmunks or drones, but I soon found the offending button and asked the bartender's assistant to guard the stereo while I danced.

That seemed to solve the music problems, but then money started to disappear from my purse in the dressing room. If I started dancing with US $50 in my purse, I would return to find $40. It happened so often and so predictably that I was able to catch the thief red-handed: a bus boy, the one with the sweetest disposition and the most innocent personality.

An unusual incident happened one night. The chef always sent us orange juice after we finished our performances. One evening, my juice contained broken glass instead of crushed ice. Nobody could explain how it got there, but I wondered if the discrepancy in my pay scale, at US $350 a week, and that of other employees, who averaged only $100 a month, could have caused enough jealousy to do this. I never discovered the culprit or his motivation.

Between price haggling Hassan, gossiping musicians, a sabotaging secretary, a thieving bus boy and booby-trapped juice, I began to feel like I needed a friend. When a statuesque dancer from New Mexico arrived I was vastly relieved.

Dianne had a magnificent mane of long red hair; she wasn't particularly tall, but she loved high heels and she towered over compact Colombian men like a mythical Amazonian tribeswoman. She and I got along beautifully, which annoyed the temperamental Mohammed, who then refused to rehearse. Dianne and I decided that we would have to limit ourselves to solos, until Hassan insisted that we synchronize our performances at least once a night (yet he did nothing to induce cooperation from the cantankerous Mohammed). How can two dancers, who have never met before, dance a synchronized duet without ever hearing their music? It seemed impossible. Our only choice was to tap into our intuition and improvise our duets every night.

As with comics, who can hone their skills brilliantly in improvisational theatre, unrehearsed shows night after night can develop formidable skills in a dancer. Recently, for a stage performance before a sold-out audience, I was asked to improvise a five-minute solo to a live Arabic drummer as he stood on center stage playing a set that I had never heard in my life.* When one of my students later asked me how I managed to hit every single accent the instant he played it, I pointed to years of experience with people like El Khalifa's pesky Mohammed.

*See "Emerald Dreams" concert video, pg. 168.

An interesting array of famous performers (on the belly dance circuit) crossed my path while in Bogotá.

Horacio Cifuentes, who danced with the San Francisco Ballet, helped to forge a place for men in the world of belly dance. When he applied his spectacular talents to interpret belly dance for men, he quickly gained fame and was crowned "Mr. America of the Belly Dance." Cifuentes was born and raised in Cartagena and, when he came to Bogotá to visit his father, he offered daily classes at an upscale dance studio. Of course, I took his classes every day for a month!

Vince Delgado, an active musician in the San Francisco Bay area and a successful recording artist, became our drummer for a time.

The late "Amir," a fantastic male dancer from Boston, would have worked with us, but Hassan hit the roof when Amir asked for $700 a week. I refused to try talking the legendary Amir into Hassan's insulting pay suggestions.

"Amaya," another nationally known workshop instructor, then living in Austin, Texas, was one of the Libano's near misses. She was part of a group that Mr. Zeytun double booked; I wondered if he knew, when he cancelled without explanation, that he had ditched a very popular dancer with a huge following.

26

I soon got my chance to negotiate with Mr. Zeytun—this time, on equal footing.

Colombia's never ending sea of paperwork and corruption gave me plenty to do. Since I was the only one that knew the ropes, Hassan told me to do the paperwork for all his performers, dragging them from office to office every week to visit lethargic officials who kept creating new difficulties, in hopes that we would give them a bribe.

"Sit over there," a puffy little official would order.

I sat, he disappeared.

"Who are you?" a man in a rumpled uniform would ask. I explained my mission, but Rumples vanished. A fat man with a handlebar mustache poked his head in to ask for documents already submitted in quadruplicate; short women in cheap suits chattered in hallways; high-handed officials wearing low-fashion pants looked for visitors who seemed too cheerful.

Hassan always arrived for our appointments at least three hours late, but that didn't make any difference because no progress was ever made during the morning. Nonetheless, officials required me to arrive exactly on time, only to sit there all morning doing nothing. Government officials kept coming up with urgent, newly invented details to perfect our paperwork.

"Lift your hair!" instructed a diminutive martinet in his baronial manner. He proceeded to write down a detailed description of one dancer's ears.

Meanwhile, back at the Libano, Mr. Zeytun had arranged for Azuri to return. She brought along Victor, a male belly dancer, and we all moved into the same little apartment building. I remembered how Mr. Zeytun had acted like he owned me, and still smarted from his refusal to pay my exit taxes—but soon I would get my chance to step up to the negotiating table with my former boss, this time, on equal footing.

Bribes, for some reason, weren't working, and Mr. Zeytun didn't have me to fill out forms for him. Finding a document he'd overlooked, government officials closed his show down completely. He tried to approach me through an intermediary, as was his custom, but I refused to discuss anything at all unless Mr. Zeytun talked to me personally.

"Tami, yes, how are you?" Mr. Zeytun asked, all charm and bright smiles. "And are you busy?"

He knew, of course, that I worked for his competitor.

"I'm dancing at El Khalifa."

"How nice—you know, I like your dancing. You are very good."

I waited.

"Ah, you know, perhaps my customers would like to see you dance again. You would like to make a little extra money, no?"

"You mean because all your dancers had their paperwork revoked? I heard they shut you down."

"Ah, that, um, just a temporary thing, you know. But perhaps you can dance for me until I resolve this little matter," he suggested.

"I already have a job."

"Please. Help me out."

"Why?"

"I need, er, that is, I will pay you well. You can come to the Libano between shows at El Khalifa."

"It'll cost you double," I said, modeling my negotiations after troublesome taxi drivers I had met while on the road.

"Oh, double, that is too high. I can pay you a *little* more."

"Double."

His upper lip began to perspire.

Whoever talks first loses, I thought.

"All right," he conceded, finally.

"And I'll need a chauffeur to drive me back and forth."

For a short while, I became the highest paid belly dancer in Bogotá, and the most pampered. I earned it—one day I did eight shows.

Dallal

*I guess we had a bunch
of little spats
with Mafiosos ...*

27

Some of the Mafiosos had money but no manners, yet they were coddled like kings.

Once I took off my finger cymbals to dance with my sword. These little instruments are about three inches (7.5 cm.) in diameter with ring-like straps sized to fit a thumb and middle finger. They are often made of precious metal, acoustically shaped to clang with an enchanting resonance if you open them quickly after clapping them together.

"I know how to play them," said one of the low-lives. He held out his hand imperiously, motioning me to lend them to him.

I had taken a dislike to him at once, but not wanting to make any trouble I let him play with the finger cymbals (out of rhythm and on the wrong fingers) while I sword-danced. When I finished, the cymbals were gone.

"Give them back please."

He smirked. "I don't have them."

What a spoiled brat. "They don't belong to me. They belong to Dianne, and I need them back!" I said.

"I saw him slip them into his girlfriend's boot," said one of the customers.

But he wouldn't return the cymbals. Dianne cried. The

cymbals were a limited edition, and quite valuable, but it was the emotional loss that triggered her tears. She had danced with those cymbals for most of her career.

"We'll call the police," I said.

"Then you'll be in trouble and this restaurant will suffer!" By now everyone was staring at him, but the Mafioso just glared.

Hassan pulled me aside and pleaded. "Forget about it. I don't want him coming back to burn my restaurant down." We never got Dianne's cymbals back, but nevertheless, Hassan gave the mannerless Mafioso free dinner and drinks all evening.

When you are young, and life is filled with humdrum events like buying a bag of oranges or waiting for a bus, you don't always see the intensity of dramas that play out around you. Had I known that while I vented my anger on that cymbal thief, President Betancur was describing a group of Mafiosos as "an organization stronger than the state"—or, if any of us knew, while we danced at El Khalifa and the Libano, that an official meeting was taking place where Mafiosos were offering to *pay off the Colombian national debt* in exchange for ... I hate to think what, I might not have made such a fuss about finger cymbals. And we probably wouldn't have carried out that little vendetta against an annoying drug trafficker who lived in our building, a mini-Mafioso known as "The Doctor."

"The Doctor" kept us awake all night long with his wild parties. Nobody could sleep, and nobody—including the owners of the building—would complain, because they were afraid.

Victor and I had first come to know each other at Mid-Eastern dance conventions in Florida, and we quickly became good buddies in Colombia. Instead of using the front doors to enter our apartments, we used to climb out our windows and walk across the roof, popping in through each other's windows for visits. Victor volunteered to help teach "The Doctor" a lesson.

Since my bathroom was connected to the room where the drug dealer slept, our plan was to collect neighbors and friends to make a racket at the bathroom door while "The Doctor" tried to sleep. We played Arabic music loud enough to deafen a jaded punk rocker; thumped tambourines and clashed finger cymbals; we sang, and best of all, we shrilled a chorus of *zaghareets* (noisy high-pitched party ululations). After waking "The Doctor" up, we'd wait quietly until he fell asleep again and then resume the pandemonium.

"What are you people doing?" he finally asked, in exasperation. He tried calling the night manager, who pleaded unsuccessfully with us to stop. The night manager was worried about two things: 1) retaliation, and 2) losing his job. In that order.

Finally, overtaken with immaturity, Victor and I decided to toilet-paper the drug dealer's door. To top it off, Victor found a rotten banana and hung it with a string. Dianne put a dollop of whipped cream on the banana and when the mini-Mafioso opened his door to complain again, he walked right into it. "The Doctor" moved out the next day.

Compared to drug traffickers, guerrilla revolutionaries are downright warm and fuzzy. Shortly before I arrived in Colombia, drug traffickers had organized a right-wing paramilitary group which they gave the charming name *Muerte a Secuestradores* (Death to Kidnappers). Two of the drug biggies at the time decided to punish FARC, and especially M-19, for their fund-raising tactics, i.e. kidnapping for ransom. Death squads proved handy, so the drug lords started using them on left-wing politicians and students. Other drug traffickers put together their own death squads, calling them *sicarios* (assassins). Bribes and death squads seemed to persuade a lot of guerrillas to keep quiet and influenced plenty of politicians to see things differently. But why stop there?

In 1983, the year I arrived, a newspaper journalist wrote a series of investigative pieces linking drug traffickers with government officials. He was machine-gunned to death. Later that year, *sicarios* assassinated his editor. It got worse after I left: now and then I've read a newspaper called *El Espectador*. In 1986, when it published reports on the Medellín Cartel, *sicarios* killed the paper's director. Reporters from another paper that I used to read, *El Tiempo*, fled the country after their names appeared on a death list. Over a five-year period during the 1980s, *sicarios* paid by drug traffickers assassinated at least 30 journalists.

You'd think these Mafiosos had no consciences. But a man named Hamid regularly flew into Bogotá from Maicao, a rough border town near Venezuela. After inviting his bodyguards to eat at El Khalifa, he showered us with tips and bestowed bottles of expensive French perfume upon us, claiming that he had a perfume import company (though, if he had a perfume business at all, it was his second occupation). He was a drug-runner who believed he should share his wealth, using his ill-gotten gains to build schools and medical clinics in small towns all over Colombia.

Even the Barranquilla Mafiosos—those fierce Libano patrons who looked like stereotypical gangsters from the cast of *The Godfather*—were prone to moments of tenderness. One evening, the mother of several Mafioso brothers accidentally fell down and hit her head, getting such a concussion that she actually passed out. As I watched, these brutal men transformed into a bunch of softies, clucking and fussing over her like old hens as they called for a doctor.

When I went to movies, I would see rough-looking characters crying, which is something I never see in America.

Hamid was later killed in a drug-related shootout and, before I left Colombia, events eliminated any doubts I might have had about Mafiosos' capacity for viciousness.

How do you become the King of Cocaine?

Colombia doesn't grow the most coca leaf. Colombians didn't invent cocaine "kitchens." And, but for the military coup that ousted Chilean President Salvador Allende, Colombia might not have achieved dominance at all. But when Chile's new government clamped down on criminals in 1973, herds of Chilean "chemists" fled to Colombia and helped Colombian entrepreneurs put together the best importing, processing and exporting system in the Western Hemisphere.

Biggest coca farms
1. Peru — cultivation: 515 tons
2. Bolivia — cultivation: 270 tons
3. Colombia — cultivation: 70 tons

Biggest cocaine manufacturer and distributor
1. Colombia

"I'll take you to the abandoned part of the mine," he volunteered.

28

Back in Miami, my tall, willowy friend Dottie read one thrilled postcard after the next. Raised in a globe-wandering family, perhaps she understood my fascination with faraway places better than most. Everything about Colombia consummated imaginations I had formed in childhood, of exotic people and adorable children; unusual foods and political intrigue. I wrote her of each new discovery until at last, she was persuaded to join me in Colombia for a short stay.

I was eager to take her to Chico, the neighborhood where I lived, where a series of tacked-together plywood stalls, roofed in plastic, showcased an astounding floral selection. Colombia ships *millions* of cut flowers around the world.

Whenever I approached this makeshift market with its panorama of colors and perfumes, a horde of small children would rush up to me. *"Ven ... ven!"* ("Come here!") Looking up at me, they would hold out a single flower.

"Un regalo para tí," they added. ("A gift for you.") Then they would lead me to their family flower stall, where again and again I yielded to the unspoken obligation to buy armfuls of fresh-cut blossoms. Beckoning me to squat down, the children would bedeck my hair with blossoms—I always had a first class collection in my hair and in my room. People said

our little apartment smelled like a funeral parlor.

Though it was fun to explore Colombian supermarkets, I just *had* to show Dottie one of the gourmet food stores in an upscale shopping mall. Who could feel anything but enticed? Slowly rotating mirrored pedestals displayed specialty foods as if they were fine Austrian crystal. Curiosity aroused, we approached to examine their delicacies, but were stopped in our tracks when we saw the display items: Cheez Whiz, Oreo cookies and Wheat Thins.

Mood music, no doubt purchased from an elevator manufacturer, played softly in the background as a clerk approached.

"Three dollars for M&Ms?" I asked.

"They're imported."

With a fancy flourish, the clerk brought out gift boxes, unwrapping delicately colored tissue paper to reveal ... Doritos, Hershey bars and canned Spam.

"Never mind—it's out of my price range," I said, and we beat a hasty exit. The real gourmet treat was "market day" in any of the small towns surrounding Bogotá.

Zipaquira

Eager to share Colombia with Dottie, I took her to Zipaquira, a small town near Bogotá known for its salt mines.

It was Tuesday, market day in Zipaquira, and virtually the

whole town turned into an open-air grocery store. Fresh produce covered the plaza and all the nearby streets. From tables and stalls, farmers sold vine-ripened fruits, far sweeter than those in the USA, which are picked green and ripened on a truck; and crunchy crisp vegetables. Fishes in baskets stared up at us as we examined homemade cheeses. Special Colombian cheese bread, freshly baked, wafted delicious scents as we passed by. We stocked up on fresh berries and homemade cheese, gorging ourselves with exotic fruits before setting out to see the sights.

Fruit slime and eyeball juice

Colombia positively gushes with exotic fruits.

Curuba looks like a pickle full of slime. Its black seeds crunch when you eat them.

Tomatos de Arbol (tree tomatoes) are hard on the outside and taste tomatoey; you scoop out the pulp and blend it with milk and sugar to make shakes.

Maracuya (passion fruit) is mainly used for its tart juice.

Ciruelas, "plums," are not round, but oblong, and orange, and have a big seed in the middle.

Guanabana (soursop) is a big green fruit with sickeningly sweet white goo inside. It's used in desserts and juices.

Mamones—we called them eyeballs—are grape-sized round fruits. You pop the skin with your teeth and suck the tasty, sour white fruit which clings tenaciously to a large seed.

The Zipaquira salt mine, gouged into an immense subterranean structure four tiers deep, supports the town's economy and supplies salt to much of South America. The most unusual part of the mine is a huge all-salt underground church, a monumental tourist attraction with balconies, domed chambers and labyrinthine staircases, on Sundays echoing solemn spiritual chants—the pillar of religion for the population of Zipaquira, where most of the men work in the mines. Below the cathedral were working salt mines; above it, abandoned tunnels.

"If you touch the polished walls and then lick your fingers, you can taste the salt," I said, watching a man out of the corner of my eye as he approached. He wore a miner's hat, khaki shirt and construction boots.

He walked right up to us, offering a friendly smile. "I am a miner. My name is Francisco," he said. "Do you want to see the mines? I can take you."

"Do they let us visit while they're working?" I asked.

"No, but I'll take you to the abandoned part," he volunteered.

Dottie and I whispered together, wondering if he expected money. Or sex. Logic would caution us against going with this man, but I had a good feeling and trusted him. As Francisco led us through dark passageways, however, we realized this was an excellent way to get kidnapped or killed, and vowed to stay on guard. The lonely tunnels blanketed us in a shroud of utter darkness.

Then Francisco turned on the lamp on his miner's helmet and began to tell us stories about his beautiful wife and children. Except for the feeble glare from Francisco's helmet, we could see nothing at all, until by and by, dim slivers of light appeared from the church below, glimmering through spaces among the wooden boards where we walked.

Despite Francisco's gentle ways, Dottie grew uneasy. "If he decided to attack us with a knife," she whispered, "we'd be defenseless."

Suddenly, the darkness burst into soft white cottonballs. This explosion of utter blackness into eccentric white salt was so bizarre that, had we stepped right into an unusually eery science fiction painting, the effect could not have been more fantastic.

To this day, having traveled to hundreds of remote and unusual locations, the abandoned tunnels of the Zipaquira salt mine stand out as one of the most surreal places I've ever been. Francisco proudly escorted us back to the entrance, refusing to take any money. He had wanted nothing more than to see our astounded faces when he switched on a light. "You should come back during the miners' festival," he said. "Now *that's* an experience!"

"I'll try," I said, and took his address, really wanting to return.

29

Bombs exploded.
People were arrested.
Two armed policemen
stopped us on the street.

In 1984, the drug wars in Colombia escalated. Mafiosos and drug dealers had seemed to enjoy a high position in society and their money bought them respect—until drug runners shot down a government minister on the street.

Though I equated Barranquilla Mafiosos with brutality, by 1984 the Medellín criminal network had eclipsed Barranquilla's reputation for ruthlessness. Under the leadership of the infamous Pablo Escobar, the Medellín Cartel graduated from small-time smuggling into massive airlift operations, complete with radar and sophisticated electronic communications.

Rodrigo Lara Bonilla, Colombia's Minister of Justice, had launched a courageous effort to eradicate the drug cartels. Just after a successful raid on the massive Tranquilandia drug complex, narcoterrorists exploded the rear window out of his white Mercedes with a MAC-10 machine pistol, killing him instantly. President Betancur immediately invoked a state of siege. Civilians were forbidden to carry weapons, and patrons at the restaurant stopped parking their guns on the tables. Police began to stop and search anyone, any time, for any reason.

Walking home one night with my friend Delio (the Libano's doorman), and his brother, two heavily armed policemen stopped us. "*No mueve!*" the taller one barked.

("Don't move!") As he motioned for Delio to submit to a full body search, I instinctively reverted to innocent, carefully-modulated tones to keep things calm. Though they searched Delio and his brother from head to toe, they seemed less concerned with me, searching only my bag. This incident didn't feel much different than Miami, where police stopped people like me quite often, usually out of curiosity caused by my costume, or because Putt Putt had putted too loud.

Bombs exploded. People were arrested. Few people seemed to care. Whenever I asked about the incidents, people said simply, *"No importa."* Perhaps it was apathy, or perhaps it was a sense of futility.

With the assassination of Lara Bonilla, narcotics traffickers made their intentions perfectly clear: *If you are in office, or if you are campaigning for office, you had better not take a position against drug traffickers.* Not only did drug lords bully and bribe politicians—in some areas they were becoming so powerful that they elected *themselves* to local or state office.

We went about our daily lives with little discussion of these issues. Newspapers scarcely mentioned the mushrooming drug cartels' poisonous activities; politicians edited the drug issue out of their speeches; we continued to dance at night and shop the open-air markets during the day. The most noticeable changes: more rifle-toting policemen, fewer *pistolas* on the tables, and bodyguards no longer carried their ubiquitous "briefcases."

30

Dogs need to have some finesse in a restaurant—once, a St. Bernard deposited a big pile of slobber next to my spaghetti.

Arequipe

While walking downtown, Dianne and I expounded on the glories of *arequipe*, the national dessert of Colombia. *Arequipe* is made by cooking milk and sugar until it thickens into a sensuous pale orange caramel. Colombians eat it with white cheese or candied figs; I like it best with bread or fresh strawberries.

We happened upon a man selling puppies on the street. They were so little and cute—he promised they wouldn't grow— and I had given my teddy bear away the week before to a little girl who really wanted him, leaving me with nothing to hug.

The puppy-seller showed us one wiggling little dollop of caramel that matched Dianne's coat, a diminutive fuzzball just the color of *arequipe*. We pooled our money and bought the puppy, naming her—of course—Arequipe. Wherever we went she went too: to restaurants, on the bus, to government offices. People oohed and cooed. My friend Germán adored Arequipe and sometimes stuffed her inside one of his fur-lined gloves.

We took Arequipe to tea at a restaurant. The waitress, delighted with the name as well as the puppy, pushed Arequipe around on her dessert cart, letting customers pick her up and put her on their tables to play; then she would place the puppy back on her dessert tray for another ride.

When Germán and I went to Tony Roma's, considered a high class American restaurant in Bogotá, we hid Arequipe in a basket. Any old dog can come to a casual Colombian eatery, but to go to a fancy restaurant, canines must have some finesse. I could understand that—once Dottie and I went to a nice Italian restaurant where a drooling St. Bernard deposited a big pile of slobber next to my spaghetti. I lost my appetite.

Our puppy was so quiet and well behaved that we thought she would go unnoticed, but when my steak appeared she jumped out of her basket into my lap. I quickly put a napkin over her; no good—she put her paws on the table and with the napkin still on her head, stuck her nose in my plate, just as the waiter walked by.

We waited for him to expel the dog. "This is a special day," he said. "We allow dogs and" –he looked down his nose at Germán– "people like you."

When he came to this high-class establishment, Germán had stepped out of his place. I don't know whether the remark referred to Germán's gay tendencies or to his social class. I don't think the two men knew each other well enough to have anything personal against each other. Though my dog was welcomed, Germán was merely tolerated. Oh well. So much for *that* waiter's tip.

Arequipe's fur gradually changed from caramel to beige,

no longer resembling the dessert that was her namesake. I took some of the henna Dianne used on her hair and dyed Arequipe, but she came out the color of orange crush, looking ridiculous.

Arequipe (Colombian Caramel)

All that's addictive in Colombia is not white. Here is a recipe that may increase your cavities:
Arequipe

3 liters whole milk (2.1 quarts)
2 pounds sugar
Pinch of salt
Pinch of baking soda
1 stick of cinnamon

Without stirring, bring all ingredients to a boil in a large pot, preferably made of copper. Lower heat and cook, stirring occasionally with a wooden spoon until sauce turns a caramel color and thickens.

Serve alone or eat with bread, soda crackers, fruit or fresh cheese. Or, use as a filling in cakes or cream puffs.

Gunfire crackled.
I locked myself in a room
while the bullets flew.

31

A time for leaving

The political climate in Colombia grew steadily worse. Danger was no longer limited to Colombian officials. The USA had begun to extradite Colombian drug bosses to stand trial, triggering promises by drug lords to kill two Americans for each Colombian extradited. When Betancur allowed the USA to extradite thirteen drug dealers, U.S. citizens, taking Mafioso threats at face value, returned home in droves.

Narcotics traffickers organized new death squads to dissuade people from cooperating with extradition policies, calling the punishment squads "The Extraditables." Anyone who helped enforce extradition warrants in any way was murdered. When the Colombian Supreme Court decided to gut the extradition treaty, no one was surprised.

We packed our bags and prepared to head home. Like Mr. Zeytun, Hassan had to pay exit taxes on us before we could leave Colombia, but Hassan had his own methods: he liked to claim his performers did something wrong so he could demand that the government deport them.

"No way I'll leave Colombia in disgrace," I told Hassan.

"The *only* way you'll leave Colombia is in handcuffs!" he retorted.

I knew I could get out of the country if I accepted his terms (criminal deportation), but—despite Colombia's political turmoil—I could not accept a trumped-up deportation that would prohibit me from visiting ever again, just to help Hassan. Besides, I had already learned that I could assert my right to go where I wanted, when I wanted.

Hassan's deportation strategy for Dianne and me seemed to center on a tape recorder. Ever since her finger cymbals were stolen, Hassan and Dianne had been conducting a running feud. She insisted that Hassan reimburse her, since it happened in his restaurant; he refused; she borrowed a tape recorder from the restaurant and then held it for ransom, demanding payment for her finger cymbals. Both of them insisted that I translate as they tried to negotiate a truce. Then Hassan's wife came up with a suggestion: since I was doing the translating, she reasoned, Hassan ought to make *me* responsible for the tape deck. I had no use for this cheap piece of electronics, but paranoid Hassan became convinced that I harbored a secret plan to skip the country with his tape deck. He used this idiotic little squabble as "justification" for refusing to pay our exit taxes.

Unable to work and running out of money, I visited the American Embassy to ask for help. The embassy looked like a

Dallal

huge prison, made of cold gray steel with bars everywhere
and many guards. Terrorists were always putting car bombs
outside the embassy, but that didn't seem to thin out the long
lines of people waiting for visas. By the time I finally made
my way to the front of a very long line, I discovered that the
consul had hurried back to the United States leaving no one
but guards and secretaries, who couldn't help me at all.

It was nearing 1985, and I had now been in Colombia for
almost a year. A group of Barranquilla Mafiosos contacted me
to ask if I could entertain them at a New Year's party, and
since my only interesting pastime was trying to get out of
Colombia, I accepted. I traveled to Barranquilla to dance for
the very people that made Mr. Zeytun sweat and scurry,
wondering if I'd ever get home.

When I first arrived in Barranquilla, I stayed in the home
of a family who worked for one of the drug smuggler's
legitimate businesses. Scratching around the tiny courtyard in
the midst of their small modern home was a turkey, and,
missing little Arequipe, I contented myself by playing with
him during my stay. On the morning before New Year's Eve, I
wandered out to the courtyard to visit the turkey—but he was
gone! They had killed him for dinner, and then, because they
had so many lambs, which they also killed and ate, they just
stuck my friend in the freezer. That started my first attempt at
vegetarianism, though it only lasted a week.

The driver came to take me to the drug baron's opulent

mansion. As we drove up, I decided that it resembled a giant ice cube; built entirely of white marble, it was cubic, super-modern and cold. One doesn't usually describe simplicity as "overdone," but clearly these Mafiosos had allowed their designer to take his concept as far as he wanted. Inside were ludicrously large rooms with sparse furnishings and oceans of empty space. I danced in a gargantuan living room and had no difficulty maneuvering around occasional sumptuous couches and coffee tables. Midnight approached.

Ka-pow! The noise made me shudder. When I was little, I hated the sound of balloons popping and tried to hide when we attended fireworks displays. Here in Barranquilla, exactly at midnight, all the drug lords shot their guns into the air using live ammunition. Gunfire crackled amid an arsenal of ear-splitting fireworks. I locked myself in a room and dillydallied with my makeup while the bullets flew, telling them I had to adjust my costume before the next dance, vowing to find a way out of Colombia the moment I returned to Bogotá!

Returning to DAS, Colombia's FBI-like enforcement agency, I tried to find the man who had intimidated Mr. Zeytun into paying his taxes, hoping he could arrange an equally effective visit to Hassan. "You again?" asked Jorge, the head honcho, looking exasperated.

"Yes. This time, do you have to point guns at him? Could you just tell him to pay the taxes instead?"

"Perhaps a lighter touch will suffice." Jorge only needed a

phone call to persuade Hassan to hurry over to his office, where DAS officials seemed singularly unimpressed by Hassan's complaints about his tape deck, gruffly instructing him to pay. Hassan twitched nervously.

"Now, pay the taxes on *every* performer you have deported," an official ordered. Busted! Hassan was hit with a stiff tax, amounting to 40 percent of the total wages for all his foreign performers.

Hassan offered me a $100 bribe not to make any more fuss, right in front of the government agents. Then, brazenly, he turned to one of the DAS officials.

"May I borrow $100?" he asked, clearly intending to use it for my payoff. No one was surprised. Payoffs were a normal way to take care of business.

"I don't need a payoff," I said, not planning on any more troublemaking. I had permission to leave Colombia on my own terms, the only thing I wanted.

We prepared to leave. Victor held a going-away party and invited people from the American Embassy, each of whom arrived accompanied by two heavily armed United States soldiers.

32

As I stuffed a year's worth of memories into my duffel bag, I thought of Oscar. One by one all of his old friends, all the people who knew him, even the hot dog vendor, had disappeared. The connection was broken forever.

Dianne headed back to New Mexico. We filled out mounds of paperwork and got Arequipe's shots, but just when it was time for her inspection the airport veterinarian went on a coffee break and never came back. Dianne stuffed the dog in her purse and boarded the plane home. Arequipe lived a good life for 12 years in the hills of New Mexico until the gruesome end: she was eaten by the enormous dog that lived next door. Dianne has since quit dancing and opened a bed and breakfast.

The Guambianos are now fighting a new enemy. Heroin traffickers have decided that Guambia is perfect for poppy growing. Automatic weapons and bribe money are pouring into the Guambianos' ancestral home; Guambiano leaders, admitting they are ill-equipped to fight this new challenge, say drug trafficking is the most serious threat to their cultural survival since the Spanish Inquisition.

Soon after I left, drug bosses stepped up their reign of terror. Pablo Escobar, the head of the Medellín Cartel, ordered

Dallal

the murder of 231 policemen and the assassination of Luis Galán, a leading antidrug presidential candidate. By 1987, drug-employed *sicarios* were assassinating political leaders at a rate of about 100 per month. The USA provided a $65 million package of military equipment, and Colombian military forces promptly arrested some 10,000 persons, confiscating airplanes, processing laboratories and residences.

"Better a Colombian grave," said Escobar, "than a United States prison cell." Before Escobar's grave could become a reality, he managed to wreak much more havoc. Within minutes after takeoff, an Avianca jet exploded, killing all 107 persons aboard. The cause? A bomb, planted by drug traffickers. Sixty-two more people died when a suicidal driver detonated 500 kilograms of dynamite outside the DAS headquarters in Bogotá.

Escobar surrendered in 1991 and was imprisoned. In July 1992, I brought a group of dancers and musicians to perform a two-week stint at Medellín's Hotel Intercontinental. The day after we arrived, Pablo Escobar escaped from his prison nearby, and suddenly our hotel swarmed with reporters from all over the world.

Escobar was finally executed in 1993. Upon the demise of the Medellín Cartel, more than 100 mini-cartels filled the void; it is said that nobody can control the "kids" who run them. The preeminent cocaine cartel in the world is now the Calí Cartel, described by prominent law enforcement officials as "the most powerful criminal organization in the world, perhaps in the *history* of the world."

Colombia's ability to cast a powerful spell was demonstrated clearly when the beautiful Azuri, despite all the turmoil, decided to live there permanently. She ended up facing even worse bureaucratic problems than I did; they deported her, and she lost all of her painstakingly beaded costumes.

My friend Victor, with whom I had scampered across rooftops and harassed "The Doctor," married his dance partner and returned to Central Florida, where he now teaches ballroom dancing.

The FARC guerrilla group signed a cease-fire agreement shortly before I left Colombia and, soon afterward, established a mainstream political party, the *Unión Patriótica* (Patriotic Union), known as UP. Narcotics powermongers haven't made it easy for UP to establish political strength. Right-wing death squads, continuing a long-standing feud with FARC, are blamed for assassinating at least 550 UP members. UP ran a candidate for president in 1986. He was murdered.

Lucho moved to New York City, where he attempted to further his career as a filmmaker. When I visited him a few years ago, he was totally spaced out, unreachable. I have no idea what caused him to become so disoriented, but I do know from my own experiences that New York City can push sensitive, talented souls into oblivion, sometimes through drugs, but sometimes it can induce minds to fold themselves into convolutions of their own making. I hope Lucho has moved into a full-time career in the film world, as he dreamed he would, but I have worried about him. Being raised as a rich boy in Colombia's laid-back environment does little to offer an artist the extra guts and *chutzpah* most people need to forge a career in New York City.

It seems that Karim continued to appeal to his co-performers about as much as a severe fungal infection. I heard that he put together a troupe of performers in Mafioso-ridden Barranquilla, who then abandoned him; they went on strike and left him to fend for himself. Years later in the USA, while swapping stories with a friend about performing turds we have known, my friend mentioned a violinist that he found particularly unbearable. After several funny but thoroughly obnoxious stories I found out the offending violinist was ... Karim.

What about Mr. Zeytun? Shortly after the drug wars escalated, he left Colombia. I've heard that he relocated to Washington D.C.

The brother of our bodyguarded friend, Khasif, was imprisoned shortly after the drug siege began. Khasif left Colombia soon afterwards.

Sheeba, the Miami dancer who talked me into my Colombian adventure, moved to Grand Cayman in the Caribbean and organized a successful national ballet company.

My friend and mentor Kaaren, the opera singer who sang in 18 languages throughout the world, who showed me how to put together flyers, resumes and business cards, has retired from professional singing and now works with the Miami City Ballet in an administrative capacity. We remain close friends to this day.

As for me, Colombia whetted my curiosity. I don't know the explanation for my spiritual bond with Colombia, but I know that it is unique—I have never experienced similar "memories" in any of my other travels.

I went on to visit 31 countries during the next 12 years. The world sometimes seemed cruel and at times I felt lonely and isolated. During such times, I dreamed up an imaginary dog, one that I bought on the street, a tiny dog that the vendor promised me wouldn't grow—a dog that grew uncontrollably to become a giant white pooch. When people gave me a hard time and I felt alone, I asked my huge imaginary friend to cause a commotion, licking some bribe-seeking official's face, or sitting on some man who acted like a pervert.

It was time to go home. Yet—the Amazon beckoned, and Brazil lay just across the border. My Colombian money had become worthless due to a currency crisis. So, trading my *pesos* for a bag of emeralds, I headed for Amazonia.

The End

(Please see following pages) —
How to help street kids
Dallal books and more

You can make a big difference.
Here are ways to help
Colombia's street children.

Reach out immediately—visit web pages,* read more about street kids, and then click "How can I help?"

Let the Children Live — "The Gamines"
http://www.btinternet.com/~lcl/xintro.htm

Children's Christian Fund International:
http://www.charity.org/ccf.html

European Network on Street Children Worldwide (ENSCW):
http://www.knooppunt.be/~enscw/

International Save the Children Alliance:
http://www.savechildren.or.jp/alliance/

Casa Alianza: http://www.casa-alianza.org/child2.html

UNICEF: http://www.unicef.org/

Human Rights Watch Children's Rights Project/Americas:
http://server.gdn.org/ftp/Human_Rights_Watch/Colombian_children

Street Kids International:
http://www.web.net/~ski/petermessage.html

* If you aren't online yet, order Dallal's FREE Colombia report for telephone numbers and addresses of organizations that help children

Dallal books and more . . .

Look for all of the Tamalyn Dallal books at your local bookstore. Suggestion: bring along the "ISBN number" (included below) in case your local store has sold all their copies; they will gladly special order for you! Or, use the order form on pg. 169 — or call, e-mail, fax, or visit our web site to order.

Books by Tamalyn Dallal:

They Told Me I Was A Man: **A Young Woman's Multicultural Adventures in BRAZIL** U.S. $14.95 **ISBN #: 1-890916-20-X**

Dallal arrives in Brazil via the Amazon Jungle equipped only with a duffel bag, talent, and a bag of emeralds. While meandering through northern Brazil, she sidesteps a variety of perverts, only to encounter police whose behavior is even more depraved — they insist they must "investigate" her gender.

In BRAZIL, Dallal guides you to street urchins who organize to form a successful political lobby; shows you a cringe-full of animal cruelties; joins a crowd of dazed carnavál street partiers and takes you behind the scenes into Sao Paulo's rich and gentrified Arabic community.

They Told Me to Break the News: **A Young Woman's Multicultural Experiences in CUBA** U.S. $19.95 **ISBN #: 1-890916-21-8**

An extraordinary true story with an intensely personal perspective on Cuban-American events. While Dallal is evolving from a disenchanted VISTA worker into an accomplished night club performer, a Cuban friend is murdered in Miami. Someone, it is decided, must tell his mother that her child is dead. On a rare Humanitarian Visa, Dallal goes to Cuba to break the news.

Dallal's compassion for kids in desperate circumstances reemerges when she returns from Cuba and takes in a Cuban-American teenager, who soon dons glittering costumes and learns Mid-Eastern dance, listens to Snoop Doggy Dogg, worries about her mother (rehab) and her father (prison). In an endeavor to connect her foster daughter with a more extended family tree, Dallal arranges for a second visit to Cuba, this time to break the news that a child is *alive*.

(over)

Dallal books . . . continued

They Told Me My Passport Was Fake: A Young Woman's Multicultural Adventures in ALGERIA, TUNISIA AND MOROCCO U.S. $14.95 ISBN #: 1-890916-22-6

After a decade of sequined-but-strange travel experiences in Latin America, Dallal whirls into a new, more mature, and (she hopes) safer itinerary. Following a brief-but-tempting encounter with a handsome Algerian Berber and years of cultural research on the Middle East, Dallal cannot resist a trip to North Africa in search of (1) a remote matriarchal tribe whose women have been banned from mainstream Muslim society and (2) the opportunity, albeit unlikely, to bump into a certain handsome gentleman.

Soon she discovers just how complicated it can be for a young woman to travel alone into certain parts of the world. With her unique blend of grace, wit and spicy socio-political perspective, Ms. Dallal will escort you to an ancient world fragmented into struggling governments, twentieth-century conflicts, and jewel-studded night life.

Special Reports by Tamalyn Dallal

How to Get Started as an Entertainer: Get Noticed, Get Booked and Get PAID **Talion # 090816-19-S** U.S. $9.95

Fabulous Foods from the Travels of Tamalyn Dallal (includes recipes!) **Talion #090816-20-P** U.S. $9.95

How to Write Your OWN Travel Memoirs **Talion #090816-21-E**

Welcome to the World of Belly Dance! A Guide to Getting Started **Talion #090816-21-C** U.S. $9.95

Videotapes

Emerald Dreams (Mid-Eastern Dance Concert Video featuring Dallal and ensemble; includes drum improvisation and sword dance) **Talion #190816-19-V** U.S. $29.95

Begin to Belly Dance: A Celebration of Feminine Self-Expression (Instructional video by Dallal)
(English version) **Talion #190816-20-I** U.S. $39.95
(Portuguese version) **Talion #190816-20-D** U.S. $39.95

Picture Yourself Belly Dancing (Instructional video by Dallal) **Talion #190816-21-E** U.S. $39.95

Audiotapes

Learn the Finger Cymbals (instructional audiotape by Dallal) **Talion # 290816-19-A** U.S. $9.95

FREE Report! Dallal's update on COLOMBIA. Includes: Travel tips and itinerary; information on Colombian music; expanded contact list for helping street kids, and news updates. Use this order form to request your FREE report!

How to order from Talion Publishing: (choose one)
1. Complete this form and mail w check or credit card info to:
   Talion Publishing
   330 SW 43rd St. Suite K-547; Renton Washington 98055, USA
2. Complete this form and FAX to 1-425-228-3965. Include VISA/MC
   credit card information.
3. E-mail the item numbers you wish. Include VISA/MC credit card
   number and expiration date. E-mail: talion@ix.netcom.com
4. For secure online ordering, visit web site and use online order form:
   http://www.talion.com
5. Or call (toll free in USA: 1-888-232-1787) or 1-425-228-7131

SHIP TO (NAME): _____

PHONE: _____ **FAX** _____

ADDRESS _____

_____

E-MAIL _____

_____ **Check is enclosed (-or-)** _____ **Please bill my credit card:**

___ **VISA** ___ **MC #** _____ **Exp. Date:** _____

How Many?

___1-890916-19-6 They Told I Couldn't (COLOMBIA) ($14.95 each + $3 S&H)
___1-890916-20-X They Told Me I Was A Man (BRAZIL) ($14.95 each + $3 S&H)
___1-890916-21-8 They Told Me to Break the News (CUBA) ($19.95 e. + $3 S&H)
___1-890916-22-6 They Told Me My Passport Was Fake ($14.95 each +$3 S&H)
___090916-19-S How to Get Started as an Entertainer ($9.95 each + $2 S&H)
___090916-20-P Fabulous Foods from the Travels of Tamalyn Dallal ($9.95 e. +$2
              S&H)
___090916-21-E How to Write Your OWN Travel Memoirs ($9.95 e.+ $2 S&H)
___090916-22-C Welcome to the World of Belly Dance! ($9.95 e. + $2 S&H)
___190916-19-V Emerald Dreams Dance Concert Video ($29.95 e. + $5 S&H)
___190916-20-I (English) Begin to Belly Dance instructional video ($39.95 each
              + $5 S&H)
___190916-20-D (Portuguese) Begin to Belly Dance instr. video ($39.95 each +
              $5 S&H)
___190916-21-E Picture Yourself Belly Dancing instr. video ($39.95 e. + $5 S&H)
___290916-19-A How to Play the Finger Cymbals instr. audiotape ($9.95 each +
              $2 S&H)
___990916-19-F Dallal's FREE Update report (COLOMBIA) (No charge)

TOTAL: U.S.$ _____ plus $ _____ shipping/handling
        (**[except in CANADA] add $10 S&H for international shipping**)

Other publications available through Talion: